He descended to the dead.
On the third day he rose again.
He ascended into heaven,
and is seated at the right hand of the Father.
He will come again to judge the living and the dead.

I believe in the Holy Spirit,
the holy catholic Church,
the communion of saints,
the forgiveness of sins,
the resurrection of the body,
and the life everlasting. Amen.

The word "creed" comes from the Latin credo meaning "I believe." The Creed is our public statement that we believe. This has been the faith of the Church down through the centuries. It is the faith of the Church throughout the world today.

Year 7

BELIEVE IN ME

ENGLISH CANADIAN CATECHETICAL SERIES

Canadian Conference of Catholic Bishops

Contents

CANADIAN CONFERENCE OF CATHOLIC BISHOPS
CONFÉRENCE DES ÉVÊQUES CATHOLIQUES DU CANADA

Dear friends,

Welcome to your new program. The prayers of all of the Canadian Bishops are with you as you begin this exploration of our Catholic faith.

This book is called *Believe in Me.* We can look at that phrase in two ways. God never stops saying to us "Believe in me. I created you and I am always with you. I will never leave you, no matter what."

We also say to God, "Believe in me. I'm trying to be a good person. I want to do the right thing. I want to understand myself and others better. I want to make a better world for all of us."

This book tries to help us understand what it means to say "Believe in me", whether it is us or God speaking. Of course, the book talks a lot about Jesus, whom God sent into our world. Jesus shows us how to believe in God. He also shows us how much God believes in us. This book also speaks of the Holy Spirit. God puts the Holy Spirit, the "force" of God, into each of our hearts to strengthen us and guide us.

All of us, younger or older, who follow Jesus and who are guided by the Holy Spirit are God's people. Together we are the Church. And so we want to show that we believe by worshipping our God and by helping and supporting each other as God wants us to do. When people look at us, they will see God who believes in us and whom we believe in.

When we think about it, God of all of the universe saying to us, "Believe in me" is really awesome. We hope that this book will help you understand just how awesome God can be in our lives.

With prayers and very good wishes for you,

The Episcopal Commission for Christian Education

Unit 1

I ... We

1.1 Who am I?

Jessie's Story

My name is Jessie. I'm new in town. I came with my dad after the mine closed down back home. There was no more work, so he came to the big city hoping to land a job.

We're staying with my Uncle Charlie until Dad can find work and a place of our own. Uncle Charlie lives alone and works shifts, so at times there is no one home but me. It's a bit scary being new and alone in a big city. Here I'm just a small fish in a big pond. I was used to being a big fish in a small pond.

Back home I had good friends who knew me and liked me for who I was. I was captain of the ball team and was even elected class vice-president once. Now I have to make all new friends and prove myself all over again.

It's a lot harder than I expected it to be. I've been through a lot of changes since my mom died, so I wasn't expecting this move to be such a big deal. I'm beginning to think that starting from scratch is tough no matter how many times you've done it. Oh well, starting again can be exciting, too. Like my dad says, "You've just got to go for it!"

Reflection questions

1. Why does Jessie say, "Now I have to prove myself all over again"?
2. Have you ever felt that you had to prove yourself in a new situation?
3. What makes new beginnings hard?
4. What makes new beginnings exciting?
5. What kinds of new beginnings have you faced?
6. How were your experiences the same as Jessie's?

A Way to Begin

When we move to a new place, go to a new school, join a new team, or just begin a new school year, we have to share who we are and learn about other people. This can be exciting: we might find a new good friend. It can also be scary: we might be rejected or feel out of place.

We can make new situations more fun and less scary if we can understand our own personalities. What makes it easier or harder for us to relate to others? Finding answers to this question will help us feel more confident and at home with ourselves.

This will make it harder for other people to drive us crazy and easier for us to get along with, and even be friends with, those who are different from us.

Think about the people you know. Do they all look the same? Probably not. For example, people are different heights. If a tall person wants a short person to see something on a top shelf, the taller person may give the shorter person a boost or get him or her a chair. A short person would not expect a tall person to walk through a low doorway without ducking. We make allowances for one another because of our physical differences.

Sometimes we forget that we also need to make allowances for our personality differences. After all, we don't all think the same way. Just as we accept that people of different heights need to do things in different ways, we must accept that people with different personalities need to do things in different ways.

The activity "What Kind of Boat Will You Take?" may help you understand different personality types and see the value and importance of each one. Your teacher will guide you through this activity.

Four Aspects of Personality

In the activity "What Kind of Boat Will You Take?" we looked at four different aspects of personality. We said that our personalities are shaped by

1. the way we sort through our thoughts;
2. the things we pay attention to;
3. the way we make decisions;
4. the way we organize our lives.

We compared each of these four things to the type of boat on which a person might choose to spend a day. The following chart sums up the different aspects of personality and the two main categories in each one.

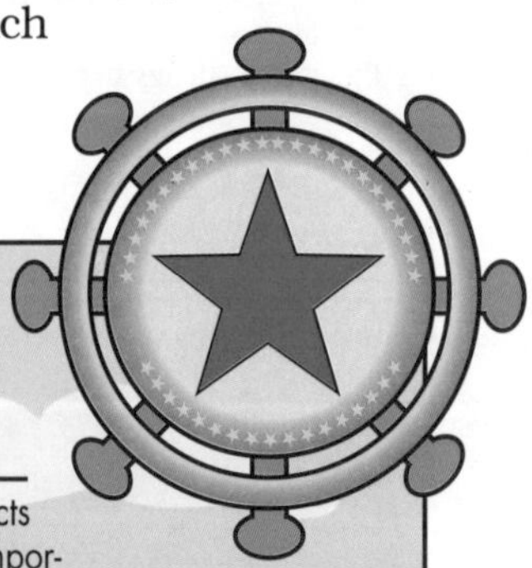

Summary Information for the

Dock Manager

Boat Sizes

(the way we sort through information)

Large: Think aloud, particularly good at group work; renew their energy by being around others.

Small: Think things through in their heads before speaking; particularly good at independent work; renew their energy by spending time alone.

Design

(the way we make decisions)

Practical: Make decisions based on facts that can be measured. Place more importance on being "right" than on being "kind."

Comfortable: Make decisions based on feelings and relationships to other people. Place more importance on being "kind" than on being "right."

Route

(the way we organize our lives)

Provide with a detailed map: Prefer structure and order; well organized.

Will go exploring: Prefer things to be open-ended; like to go with the flow; good in emergencies.

Power

(the things we pay attention to)

Motor: Pay attention to details; notice the physical details in a room, building or town, etc. but may not notice the atmosphere of the place; prefer to do things step by step; more interested in facts than theories.

Sails: Concerned more with the big picture than with the details; pay attention to the atmosphere in a room, building or town, etc., but may not notice the physical details; jump easily from one idea to another; more interested in theories than in facts.

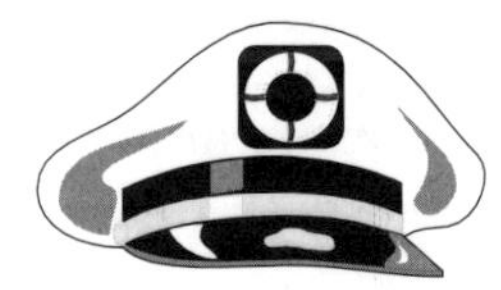

Which Type of Boat Trip Suits Your Personality?

Look at the 16 categories below to find the one that matches the results from your questionnaire (the one that is the same size, with the same power source, design, and itinerary). Read the personality description. Does this fit you? Why or why not?

Size: Small
Power: Motor
Design: Practical

1 *Itinerary:* Will go exploring

- Want to know how things work and why.
- Like to take things apart and put them back together again.
- Are usually quiet but they see the humour in life.
- Are usually calm.
- Don't get too attached to people or things.
- Prefer to do things step by step.

2 *Itinerary:* Detailed

- Know what they want or need to do and go step by step to do what needs to be done.
- Accept things as they are and don't spend a lot of time asking "what if?"
- Are not easily distracted.
- Don't waste time fooling around.
- When they begin something, they work until it is done.

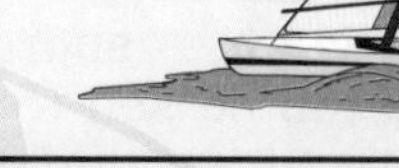

Size: Small
Power: Sails
Design: Practical

5 *Itinerary:* Will go exploring

- Like to be by themselves.
- Do well in science and math.
- Have strong opinions about what they like and don't like.
- Will argue about very small differences.
- Like to learn new things.
- Don't like parties very much.

6 *Itinerary:* Detailed

- Are very independent.
- Have strong opinions about how things should be done.
- Will do what is needed to get things done either by themselves or with others.
- Do not give up.
- Question most things and are not easily convinced to change their minds.
- Think about things in an original way.

Size: Small
Power: Motor
Design: Comfortable

3 *Itinerary:* Will go exploring

- Are happy people who usually find a way to have fun.
- Prefer to avoid too much change.
- Are quiet but friendly.
- Don't like arguments.
- Will give another person a chance even when they think the other person is wrong.
- Often prefer to let other people be in charge.

4 *Itinerary:* Detailed

- Work hard to make those they care about happy and comfortable.
- Are more interested in people than in ideas, facts or things.
- Pay attention to details and like to get things exactly right.
- Keep their promises and are faithful friends.

Size: Small
Power: Sails
Design: Comfortable

7 *Itinerary:* Will go exploring

- Care deeply about the things they are interested in, but usually only reveal their thoughts and interests to people they know well.
- Like learning and independent projects.
- Are always busy but they usually get things done.
- May seem to be off in their own world, but they are friendly once you get their attention.
- Often overlook details and what things look like.

8 *Itinerary:* Detailed

- Always try to do their best, and to do what is best for others.
- Don't give up.
- Will try new ideas if the old ones are not working.
- Seem to know what needs to be done to make the world a better place for all people.
- Are often leaders in groups working for change.
- Have a clear sense of right and wrong and they try to do what is right.

"As in one body we have many members, and not all the members have the same function, so we, who are many, are one body in Christ.... We have gifts that differ according to the grace given to us."

Romans 12.4-5

Size: Large
Power: Motor
Design: Practical

***9** Itinerary:* Will go exploring

- Are usually relaxed.
- Don't worry very much or get overly excited about things.
- Are satisfied with doing as much as they can do and leaving the rest to others or to God.
- Like to be active and learn best by doing.
- Don't like detailed explanations.
- Want to know the purpose of things before they do them.
- Often speak without thinking.
- Like to take things apart and put them back together.

***10** Itinerary:* Detailed

- Like to be in charge, and are good at organizing and running things.
- Are quick to understand how things work.
- Like to do things that clearly serve some practical purpose.
- Do not like to "waste time."
- Set realistic goals.
- Take everything one step at a time.

Size: Large
Power: Sails
Design: Practical

***13** Itinerary:* Will go exploring

- Are good at many things.
- Can talk intelligently about almost anything.
- Like to debate and can argue both sides of most issues.
- Are good at solving new and difficult problems but are often bored with daily routines.
- Are good at making what they want to do sound reasonable.

***14** Itinerary:* Detailed

- Are energetic and enthusiastic.
- Are good leaders and speakers and good students.
- Are usually well informed.
- Like to learn new things.
- When they are interested in something, they want everyone else to see how fascinating it is.
- Say what they mean.
- Are very confident and sure of themselves.

Size: Large
Power: Motor
Design: Comfortable

***11** Itinerary:* Will go exploring

- Enjoy doing almost everything and are fun to be around.
- Make friends easily with most people.
- Like to bring out the best in others.
- Like to be active, playing sports or making things.
- Are more likely to remember facts than theories.
- Have lots of common sense and they use it.

***12** Itinerary:* Detailed

- Like to do nice things for other people.
- Want everyone to get along with everyone else and do what they can to make that possible.
- Are caring, talkative and well liked.
- Are mainly concerned with people and the way things affect people.
- Have very little interest in abstract ideas.
- The more encouragement they receive, the better they do.

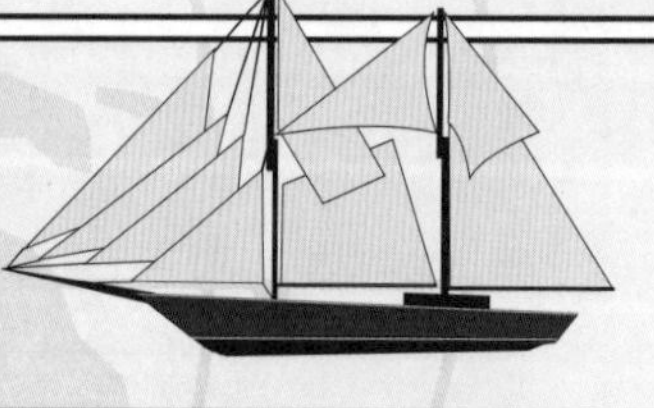

Size: Large
Power: Sails
Design: Comfortable

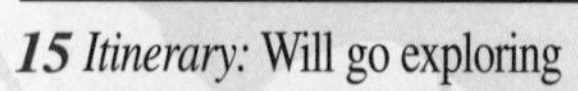

***15** Itinerary:* Will go exploring

- Are energetic, cheerful and enthusiastic.
- Are imaginative.
- Are very good at solving problems and quite willing to help others do the same.
- Don't like to plan things in advance but are good at improvising.
- Can find convincing reasons to do things their way.

***16** Itinerary:* Detailed

- Are sensitive to others' feelings.
- Are friendly and tactful.
- Are popular and usually very active in social things. But they also allow time for their school work.
- Are responsible, and will do more than they have been asked to do if that will make things run smoothly for everyone involved.

What About You?

So, what type of boat trip will you take? Will you take a large, comfortable motor boat and go exploring? Would you prefer a small, sleek sailboat and a detailed map? Or would you like something else? Each boat is suited for some types of trips and will find other types harder. In the same way, each of us has a personality that makes us the ideal person for some jobs and that makes it harder for us to do other jobs. Sometimes we get frustrated with one another because we do not see and do things in the same way. We forget that it is only the wide variety of personality types that has made it possible for human beings to do so many things.

God, in infinite wisdom, created some people who think out loud and others who prefer to think things through in their heads, some who work best in groups and others who work well on their own. God created some people with a talent for coming up with new ideas and new ways of seeing things and others who can follow ideas through and not lose sight of the details. God also created some people who can see the facts clearly and others who are more tuned in to the feelings of others. Finally, God created some of us to be well organized and others to cope well with surprises. Each kind of personality is needed in God's plan for the world. Each one of us is called to celebrate the wonderful gift of our own personality and to appreciate the goodness of personalities that are different from ours.

Relating to Others

As you read the descriptions of the personalities that went with each boat, you may have seen that more than one type seemed to describe you. You will probably find that it is fairly easy to understand people who would describe themselves as any of the types that fit you. Some descriptions probably did not fit you at all. You may find that you often misunderstand, or are misunderstood by, people who would describe themselves as one of these types. Just remember that you may sometimes need help from a person whose personality is very different from yours to work through a hard situation.

Each person is made in the image of God. That means God is revealed in each person and each personality type. Inter-acting with people who are different from us gives us a chance to understand God better. When we learn to see the goodness in all people, we learn to

When you are having trouble communicating with certain people, ask yourself what type of boat trip they would choose. How is their personality different from yours? What makes it hard for you to communicate with them? Are you convinced by facts while they are convinced by emotions? If so, you might communicate better if you tried to pay more attention to people's feelings when you were talking to this type of person. Do you tend to look at the big picture while they think about details? If so, you might communicate better if you talked about this difference and agreed that some time needs to be given to both things. What other differences can you name? What might help you get beyond them?

value the awesome nature of our God, who creates and reveals goodness in so many ways.

Doogie Dogma *(Catechism #1934)*

God has given each one of us a splendid and unique personality. We join in a psalm that is said to be from King David that praises God for creating us as we are:

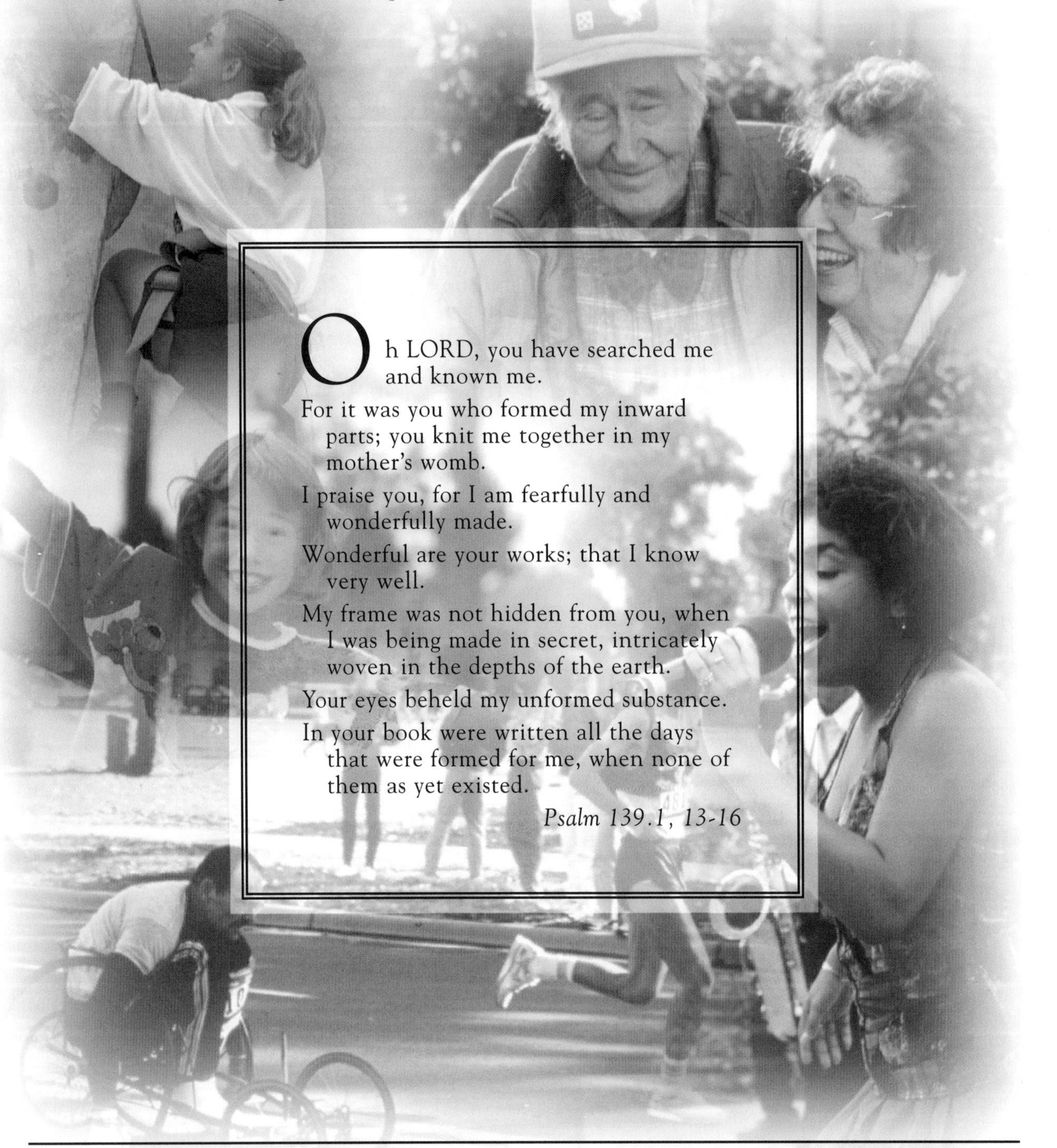

Oh LORD, you have searched me
and known me.
For it was you who formed my inward
parts; you knit me together in my
mother's womb.
I praise you, for I am fearfully and
wonderfully made.
Wonderful are your works; that I know
very well.
My frame was not hidden from you, when
I was being made in secret, intricately
woven in the depths of the earth.
Your eyes beheld my unformed substance.
In your book were written all the days
that were formed for me, when none of
them as yet existed.

Psalm 139.1, 13-16

1.2 Am I normal?

A Very Strange Visit

I'm quite glad to meet you, and please call me Sid.
I'm a perfectly normal and regular kid.
But a week ago Monday at seven at night
I had a strange visit from a small beam of light

Which slid into my room and started to speak.
My head went all funny; my knees went all weak.
"I want to be normal," I heard it say clearly.
"Will you be my teacher? You're the best, or quite nearly.

"There's no one more normal, more normal than you.
If I want to be normal, please what should I do?"
That bodiless voice was unpleasant and fright'ning.
"Well, there is your answer." The thought hit like lightning.

"If you're to be normal, a kid just like me,
Then you must have a body, one people can see."
"Yes, a body," it said, "Oh, Sid, thanks for your help."
With a "poof" he'd a body. I let out a yelp.

For there right before me – yes, right by my bed
He was standing, just standing there wearing my head!
And not only my head but my elbows and knees,
Why, that was my body! It was even my sneeze!

Yes, my sneeze. What a sound! It's one I know well.
It's a sound I've been making so long I can tell
That it's mine – my own sound from my mouth and my nose!
This just was not normal! He was wearing my toes!

I said, "This is wrong. It's not what you should do.
A body that's normal must be made for you.
You cannot copy mine. Your own must be unique,
With a voice that is yours, should you happen to speak."

He changed – not too much – he'd pass for my brother,
But Mom could at least tell us one from the other.
"That's better," I said. "Now, do you feel all right?"
He looked at me, puzzled. "I'll just feel as you might."

I had to explain, "If you're normal you feel
But the things that you feel in your heart must be real.
If your feelings have meaning they will be your own.
You can't take them from others, not even on loan."

"Own body, own feelings, will that be enough?"
"Not for normal," I said. "No, you still need more stuff.
Yes, you still have to learn how to think and decide."
Then he said, "I'll use you as my measure and guide.

"For each situation, will you make a list
Of the thoughts that are right, for each subject the gist?"
"Don't you get it?" I laughed. "You must think for yourself;
For a person is not like a book on a shelf.

"A book that's been written has thoughts that won't change.
So as time passes by some old books may seem strange.
For a book can't adapt as new truths come to light,
But a person's thoughts can; that's what's normal and right.

"You'll think some new thoughts when life's not what it was.
It's quite normal for thoughts to change as your life does.
And your life as a whole happens only to you
So your thoughts must be yours, for no others will do."

"Well, that about does it," I said with a grin.
"If I want to be normal," he said, "I'll begin
With a body that's mine that I care for and keep;
My own feelings and thoughts, my own dreams when I sleep.

"I must learn to decide what's right and what's wrong
And the song in my heart – it must be my own song."
Then I said, "One more thing that it's normal to do
Is to know you need God and a good friend or two.

"Each person who's normal to someone's connected
For we affect others and we are affected.
And the ways we're connected are unique to us.
If your friends are quite different, don't kick up a fuss.

"You're lucky, you're normal, you're unique to you.
Just keep things in balance and you'll make it through."
Then he clapped and he danced and he stood on his head,
And was gone! He's unique! "Yes, he's normal," I said.

Being Whole

The Gospel of John (10.10) tells us that Jesus came so that we might have life and have it "abundantly." To have life abundantly means to be whole. In Jesus, God invites us to be whole people and to experience the full wonder of what it means to be human.

To be whole is to be always growing and developing every aspect of ourselves. God made us whole. We stay whole by taking care of all that God has given us.

God gave us minds. Develop your mind and be whole.

There's an old story about a man who carried his front door on his back so that no one could break down the door and rob his house. The man thought he had found a brilliant solution to a problem in his town. He could not understand why his neighbours were still wasting their time trying to solve the town's crime problem.

We laugh when we hear this story and wonder who would be so ridiculous. *We* certainly wouldn't! Or would we?

Do you ever listen to only one side of a story? Do you ever take the easy way out even when this may cause other problems later? Do you always think about the effects of decisions you make? Do you ever say that you know all you need to know and that studying is a waste of time? Are you developing the mind God gave you?

God lets us choose. Learn to make good decisions and be whole.

The current and the wind were pushing our sailboat toward the rocks. We didn't have the power we needed to turn into the wind and sail away. In less than a minute, the boat would be smashed on the cliff. Then, someone grabbed the wheel and turned us straight toward the cliff! It was the right decision. With the wind coming from behind, we had enough power to make a three-quarter turn into, and then away from, the cliff. We were safe. We were safe because one person had listened to enough other sailors and had watched the way the boat responded in enough different situations to make a good decision, even when that decision seemed scary and crazy.

We are not born with the ability to make good decisions. We learn to make good decisions by listening, watching, praying, studying and analyzing the decisions we have made in the past. Are you happy with the decisions you are making in your life

right now? Are you paying attention to the people who can really help you? All of your decisions together will shape the "whole person" you become. Name some decisions kids your age are making that will shape who they become. Do you like who you are becoming? How well are you using the gift of choice that God has given you?

God gave us feelings. Express your emotions in a healthy way and be whole.

Our emotions affect our whole person. Emotions can be feelings of fear–confidence, joy–sorrow, love–hate. These emotions are not good or bad in themselves. They are normal feelings we all have. But since they affect our whole person, we must never allow them to take over. Emotions must not control our decision making.

But we must not control our emotions, either. Emotions are vital signs – if we don't know how we feel, then we don't know who we really are or what we can do. When we bury our emotions, we are not showing our true selves and we are not becoming the people God wants us to be – people who can love with our whole hearts.

Our emotions are gifts from God that make it possible for us to sense what we cannot see and to draw closer to God and other people. Our emotions can help us see decisions that need to be made. Our emotions can also add strength to decisions we have already made. Our minds and emotions must work together so that we can become mature, balanced people.

What are some healthy ways of expressing your feelings? What are some poor ways of expressing your feelings? Do you usually express your feelings in a healthy way? Do you value the gift of emotion that God has given you?

God gave us bodies. Take care of your body and be whole.

Our bodies are a wonderful gift from God. We may not have strong, athletic bodies. We may not have the bodies of models. Parts of our bodies may be imperfectly formed or may have been injured. But our bodies are still good. They allow us to express what goes on inside us and to interact with creation, with God and with one another. In other words, they allow us to be human.

Imagine that your body is a priceless treasure that belongs to God. God has asked you to care for it. If God were to call you in today and ask how well you had cared for this treasure, how would you answer? What are some ways that you harm your body? What could you do to take better care of your body?

God gave us communities. Build positive relationships and be whole.

You are part of a community – what you do is affected by other people and affects other people. Think about what happens if one person in your family or one person in your class starts snapping at everyone else for no reason at all. Soon everyone is fighting. On the other hand, if one person tries to be kind to everyone else, doesn't everyone feel a little more cheerful? We can change the attitude of the world around us by changing the way we relate to the people around us.

What do you do for your friends, family and community? Which relationships in your life are not going as well as you would like? What could you do to improve them?

God gave us a spiritual sense. Nourish your spirit and be whole.

Why do some people find it easier than others to be happy? Why are some people hopeful even when everything is going wrong? Why can some people see beauty everywhere while others see only ugliness? Because some people have grown in a spiritual way.

All people are spiritual – even those who do not know or believe in God. However, those who talk and listen to God have a stronger spiritual sense and so are more able to see beauty, have hope and feel joy. Human beings were created to know, love and serve God. Without God in our lives, we may find it hard to be happy with ourselves and with the world.

What lifts your spirit? What do you find beautiful? What reminds you of God's goodness?

God made us mortal. Know your limitations and be whole.

People can only feel whole when they accept themselves and know that they cannot control everything. In all that we do, there are limits. Limits are not all bad. Imagine a football game with no boundaries or a race with no finish line. Some of the fun and the challenge would be missing. The limits in our life help us to live with a purpose. Life is more fun when we learn to appreciate our limits and limitations and the challenges they present.

The one limit we all face is that we are mortal. We have only one life to live. By the time we die, whatever we have made of ourselves, in co-operation with God, will be "who we are." Knowing that we will die someday reminds us to live each day fully and in a healthy way.

When is it healthy to challenge limitations? When can we do more if we accept limits? What limits and limitations are hard for you to accept?

Doogie Dogma *(Catechism #167 & #193)*

1.3 Do I belong?

The Bible: Our Story

The word "bible" means "the books." Written by many different people who were guided by God's Spirit, the Bible is like a small library of books in one. It is divided into two major parts: Christians call the books written before Jesus the "Old Testament," and the ones written after he came the "New Testament." Look at the diagram on the next page to see how this "library" is set up.

The Hebrew Scriptures make up most of the Old Testament. In them, we find the story of God's love for the Hebrew people (also known as the Israelites or the Jews). These Scriptures, which were written over about a thousand years, are the basis of the Jewish faith.

The Old Testament Scriptures were the ones Jesus was taught from when he was growing up. They were also the ones that all of the apostles and the writers of the New Testament knew and believed in. Our Christian faith story is rooted in these Scriptures as well. We can trace our roots back about 4000 years!

The New Testament is the story of Jesus as he reveals God's love for us through his life, death and resurrection. It is also the story of the early followers of Jesus and how the Holy Spirit formed them into the people of God – the Church. The oldest book of the New Testament (1 Thessalonians) was written around the year 51, about 21 years after the death and resurrection of Jesus. The other books of the New Testament were written over the next 60 years.

The Bible is our story. It is about our relationship with God, and God's relationship with us, over time. It is the story of our creation in Adam and Eve, and the story of our re-creation in Jesus, when God "makes us new persons," saving us from our sins and giving us new life. The Bible is our family history. It reminds us that we come from a long line of people who have been loved and cared for by God even when they struggled, doubted and failed. The Bible is our "membership book." It reminds us that we do belong, we do fit into God's plan, no matter who we are or what we have done. Above all, the Bible is our love story because it is the story of God's deep love for each and every one of us.

The Bible, however, is much more than our individual story – it is the story that makes us a community. No one of us alone has lived the entire biblical story. No one of us has accepted all that God offers, and no one of us has perfect faith. It is only together that we have lived and keep living the whole biblical story. Together we have experienced and accepted the saving power of God in every part of life. Together we know God, and together our faith is strong and complete. God's self-revelation was not only to me or to you, to Moses or to Peter, but to all of us together: to God's people. So the Bible is *our* story. As we share it and reflect upon it together, we become one community.

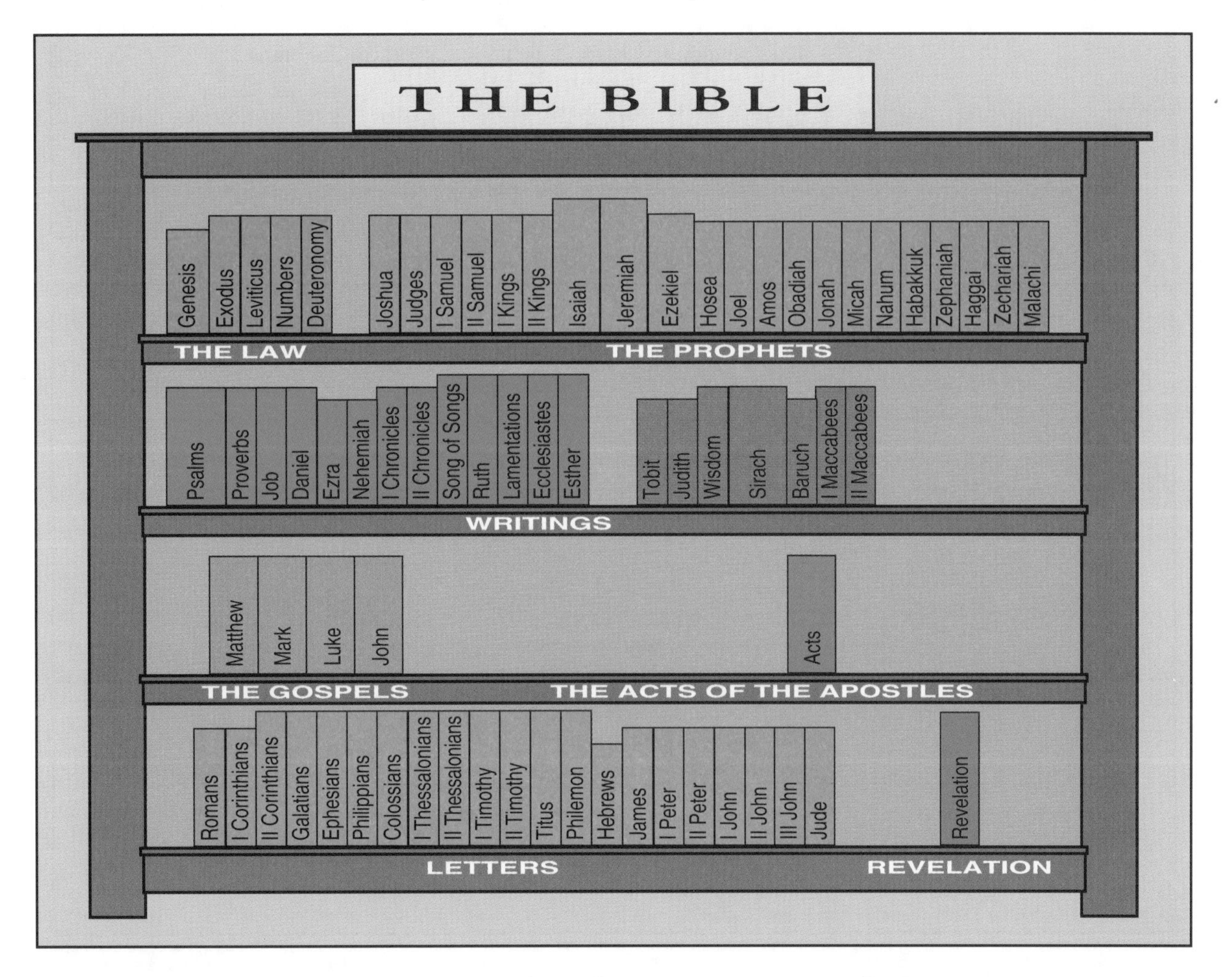

DATE	EVENT	DESCRIPTION	CONNECTION TO OUR LIVES
1800 BCE	Abraham	Our faith journey begins with the call and response of Abraham and his wife Sarah.	We are a people who have had to go many new places and begin many new things. We trust that God is with us because God was with Abraham and Sarah.
1600–1250 BCE	Settlement in Egypt	Abraham and Sarah's descendants leave Canaan and follow Joseph into Egypt. When Jacob went to Egypt, God reassured him: "I am God, the God of your Father. Do not be afraid." God reminds Jacob that just as God was faithful to Abraham and Sarah, God will always be faithful.	Even though we are a people of faith, we are often afraid. When we must make choices that affect many others, we turn to God as Jacob did. Because we know the story of the Israelites' move to Egypt, we know that God is with us even when everything in our lives is changing.
1250 BCE	Moses/Exodus	God calls Moses to lead his people out of slavery in Egypt. God makes a covenant with the Israelites in the desert at Mount Sinai.	This is our story when we feel that life is without hope. God will free us from all that oppresses us but we must make a commitment to avoid everything that oppresses others.
1250–1050 BCE	Entry into Canaan	The Hebrew people struggle to settle the land of Canaan. Even though this is the "promised land," even though it is part of God's plan for the Israelites to live in Canaan, the people must work to make God's plan a reality.	The entry into Canaan, the story told in Joshua and Judges and Ruth, is our story when we struggle to make our hopes and dreams a reality. If we want our dreams to come true, we must give God an important place in our lives.
1030–930 BCE	Kings of Israel	Saul becomes the first king. David creates a nation. Solomon builds the Temple. Some people worship idols instead of God; others reject God.	The stories of the kings are the stories of our struggle with power, control and responsibility. We must take responsibility for our lives. It is up to us to turn from things that pull us away from God and destroy us.

Note: We have replaced the terms B.C. (before Christ) and A.D. (Anno Domini) with BCE (before the Common Era) and CE (the Common Era). BCE and CE are used by many history and scripture scholars. BCE covers the same time period as B.C.; CE covers the same time period as A.D.

DATE	EVENT	DESCRIPTION	CONNECTION TO OUR LIVES
Beginning in 800 BCE	The Prophets	God speaks through the prophets and calls the people to see the destructive power of their sins. The prophets warn the people that there will be suffering if people keep ignoring God and ignoring the needs of God's children.	These words are for all of us when we turn our backs on God and God's plan for us. We are the people to whom the prophets speak. We have seen the effects of sin and injustice, yet we ignore the injustice around us. This is our warning.
587–538 BCE	Exile in Babylon	The Kingdom of Judah is brought down by the Babylonians. The Temple in Jerusalem is destroyed. All of the leading Jewish citizens are sent to Babylon. The Hebrew people no longer have a nation of their own. During the Exile, faithful Jews such as Judith helped keep the Hebrew faith alive.	This is our story when we must face the results of our actions. When we do not live as God calls us to live, the world suffers. Our communities can only survive if we live in justice and love. (See Amos 5.24.) This is our story when we see others in need and do nothing. The story of Judith, like the later story of Esther, reminds us that even during the bad times in our lives, there are things we can do to help others and stay faithful to God.
538–400 BCE	Return to Jerusalem	The Jews (from the word "Judah") return home. The Temple in Jerusalem is rebuilt. Judaism becomes a religion of Law (Torah).	This is our story as we develop a plan for becoming better people. Our plans are good as long as they draw us closer to God and one another. They become harmful when they become ends in themselves, when systems and structures are more important than God.

DATE	EVENT	DESCRIPTION	CONNECTION TO OUR LIVES
4 BCE (approx.)	Jesus' birth	Jesus is born to the Virgin Mary. God becomes human and lives among us so that we may come to understand God's love in a whole new way.	This is the promise to each of us – of hope in the midst of every darkness. It is the promise that God will always reach out to us in love.
27–30 CE (approx.)	Jesus' public ministry	Jesus teaches in Galilee and Jerusalem. He teaches people about the reign of God and he helps people to understand what it means to love God and to love our neighbours.	The Gospel stories give us guidance. The struggles of the apostles and of the women who stayed with Jesus until the end give us courage to keep going when we are afraid or when we have failed.
30 CE (approx.)	Jesus' death and resurrection	Jesus is crucified. Three days later, he rises from the dead and appears first to Mary Magdalene and then to the apostles.	This is our story of hope. This is our promise that love is stronger than hate and violence. This is our reason to care.
30 CE (approx.)	The coming of the Holy Spirit at Pentecost	God sent the Holy Spirit who gave the disciples the courage and the gifts they needed to share the good news of Jesus.	This is our reminder that God always gives us the gifts we need to do the work God calls us to do.

I could just read the Bible on my own and pray to God. There's no point to religion class.

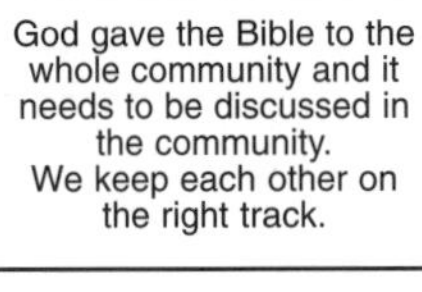

Doogie Dogma *(Catechism #113)*

DATE	EVENT	DESCRIPTION	CONNECTION TO OUR LIVES
30–110 CE	Spread of Christianity and the writing of the New Testament books	After the death and resurrection of Jesus, his followers begin to spread the good news that God calls all of us to new life and wholeness in Christ.	This is our call and our purpose in life. We are to share God's love with all those we meet. When we live in love as Jesus taught us, our lives will have meaning and joy.
49–62 CE	Paul's ministry	Paul writes to and visits newly-formed Christian communities to advise them on many issues. Even in the early church there were many struggles and disagreements about what it meant to follow Jesus.	Sometimes we get frustrated because people in the Church do not agree on issues of faith, or because people do not seem to be practising what they preach. Paul's letters help us remember that this is not a new problem, and that with faith, love and perseverance we can work things out.

Note: We have replaced the terms B.C. (before Christ) and A.D. (Anno Domini) with BCE (before the Common Era) and CE (the Common Era). BCE and CE are used by many history and scripture scholars. BCE covers the same time period as B.C.; CE covers the same time period as A.D.

Unit 1 Summary Statements

- A creed is a summary of the most important elements of our faith.
- Two creeds are very important in the Catholic Church: the Nicene Creed and the Apostles' Creed. The Apostles' Creed begins with the word "I"; the Nicene Creed begins with the word "We." This unit takes its name from the first word in each creed. These two words remind us that our faith is both personal and communal.
- All people are made in the image and likeness of God. The more we understand and value the variety among people, the more we will appreciate the vastness and wonder of God.
- God has given each person different gifts and talents because God wants us to work together. We need the insights and skills of those who are different from us.
- God wants us to be whole people. To be whole we must care for and develop these different sides of ourselves: our minds; our bodies; our spirituality; our ability to understand and express our emotions in a healthy way; our ability to make good decisions; our relationships with others; and our understanding of our own limits and limitations.
- God and the Christian faith offer us help and guidance as we try to be whole.
- The Bible is our story and the story of our community.
- The Bible is a collection of writings, inspired by God and written by many different authors over a long time. The Bible is divided into two main parts: the Old Testament and the New Testament. These two parts are divided into books. The Old Testament tells the story of God's love for the Hebrew people. The New Testament is the story of Jesus as he reveals God's love for us. The New Testament is also the story of the early Christian church.

Key Terms

image of God
gifts
wholeness
Bible
Old Testament
New Testament
community
Scripture
creed

Unit 2

We believe in God

What does it take to develop trust like this?

2.1

Whom do we trust?

Choral Reading
Based on Genesis 11.31–22.19

Part I

Chorus:
We are people with many doubts. How can we say we believe?

Reader 1:
You are descendants of Abraham and Sarah. Of course you can say, "We believe."

Chorus:
But we are not like Abraham and Sarah. They did not question their faith. We question.

Reader 2:
Have you ever really listened to the story of Abraham and Sarah?

Reader 1:
Abram...

Reader 3:
That was Abraham's original name. God changed it to Abraham when he was 99. God also changed Sarah's name. It used to be Sarai.

Reader 1:
Abram and his wife Sarai lived with Abram's father Terah in the land of Ur. Now one day Terah decided that it was time to move. He thought that the family should go to Canaan. So Terah, Abram and Sarai, and Abram's nephew Lot all packed up their things and headed out.

Reader 4:
They never made it to Canaan. Instead they stopped and stayed in a place called Haran.

Reader 1:
Some time later, God told Abram that it was time for him to continue on. God said:

God:
Go from your country and your family and your father's house to the land that I will show you. I will make a great nation of you.

Reader 5:
When God said,

God:
"I will make a great nation of you,"

Reader 5:
God was promising that Abram and Sarai would have many descendants. Now Abram was 75 years old and his wife Sarai was unable to have children. A promise like that, even from God, must have seemed a little difficult to believe.

God:

I will make your name great, so that you will be a blessing. I will bless those who bless you and curse those who curse you. In you, all families of the earth shall be blessed.

Reader 2:

The promise may have seemed strange, but Abram and Sarai trusted God. So, once again, Abram and Sarai and Lot packed up all of their things and headed for the land of Canaan.

Chorus:

A wandering Aramean was our ancestor.

Reader 5:

Yes, a wandering Aramean was our ancestor. That is the first line of the oldest passage in the Bible, the very earliest recorded statement of our faith.

Reader 8:

Our faith begins with a recognition of who we are, where we come from, and what relationships shape us.

Reader 5:

Our faith is shaped by the fact that our ancestors did not have a fixed home. They wandered and God was with them in their wanderings.

Reader 3:

When Abram and Sarai arrived in Canaan, there were Canaanites living there.

Reader 4:

These Canaanites were unjust to one another and God knew that they would not change. Eventually the injustices would grow so great that their society would fall apart.

Reader 3:

When that happened, God would give the land to people who were willing to live justly.

Reader 1:

Therefore, God said to Abram:

God:

I will give this land to your descendants.

Reader 3:

Abram built an altar to God in Canaan and then he and Sarai continued on.

Reader 2:

There was a famine in the land, so Abram and Sarai headed for Egypt.

Chorus:

A wandering Aramean was our ancestor; he went down into Egypt and lived there as a foreigner.

Reader 5:

We are descended from people who experienced loneliness and isolation and all of the doubts that go with them. God was with them in those times and God is with us.

Reader 4:

Abram knew the risks of standing out in a new place. Even his relationship with God was not enough to make him feel safe. He put God's promise of descendants and God's plans for his future to the back of his mind and tried to solve his immediate problems without involving God.

Reader 3:

Just before they reached Egypt, Abram said to Sarai:

Abraham:

I know that you are very beautiful and Pharaoh will want you for a wife. If he knows that you are my wife he will kill me. So we will say that you are my sister.

Reader 1:

Sure enough, as soon as Pharaoh heard how beautiful Sarai was, he had her brought to his house as one of his wives.

Females of the Chorus:

I wonder how Sarai felt about that.

Reader 4:

Abram received many good things from Pharaoh because his "sister" was one of Pharaoh's wives.

Reader 3:

Now Abram may not have been thinking about God's promise to give Abram and Sarai children, but God does not forget promises.

Reader 1:

God sent plagues upon Pharaoh's house because Sarai was there when she belonged with Abram. Pharaoh found out that Sarai was Abram's wife – not his sister – after all.

Reader 2:

Pharaoh was not happy with Abram. He sent Sarai back to him and then told them to leave Egypt.

Reader 4:

Once again, Abram and Sarai headed for Canaan, back to the place where Abram had built an altar to God.

Reader 1:

And once again, God spoke to Abram and promised that Abram and his descendants would have all the land that Abram could see. God said:

God:

I will make your offspring like the dust of the earth; so that if one can count the dust of the earth, your offspring also can be counted.

Reader 2:

Abram built another altar to the LORD.

Chorus:

A wandering Aramean was my ancestor. He went down into Egypt and lived there as a foreigner, few in number, and there he became a great nation, mighty and populous.

Reader 5:

We can trust God because God has proven to be trustworthy. The very fact that so many people remember Abraham and Sarah as their ancestors even after 4000 years proves that God was faithful to the promise. Who today could say the exact number of Abraham and Sarah's descendants?

Reader 4:

We know that God was faithful to Abraham and Sarah, but Abraham and Sarah did not have our advantage of hindsight. For a long time, they had a promise from God but no children. Perhaps they were beginning to wonder if God really did care about them. Maybe they were afraid that they had been fools to trust an unseen God.

Part II

Reader 1:

Then God spoke to Abram again:

God:

Do not be afraid, Abram. I am your shield; your reward shall be very great.

Reader 1:

Abram wanted more than words. He asked:

Abraham:

O Lord God, what will you give me?

Chorus:

We are like Abram. We have wondered what God will give us. Sometimes it doesn't seem worth it to trust in God.

Reader 2:

Perhaps Abram had the same thoughts, for he said to God:

Abraham:

You have given me no children. The one who will inherit from me is not even a relative.

God:

This man will not be your heir; no one but your own child will inherit from you. Look toward heaven and count the stars. That is how numerous your descendants will be. I am the LORD who brought you from Ur to give you this land to possess.

Reader 1:

Abram still wasn't convinced.

Abraham:

How can I be sure that I am to possess this land?

Chorus:

We see that even people of faith like Abraham have many questions.

Reader 3:

God told Abram to prepare a sacrifice, to bring the best of what he had and offer it to God.

Reader 4:

Abram was asked to bring a cow, a goat, a ram, a turtledove and a pigeon, one of each of the things that were most valuable to him.

Chorus:

What would God ask us to give today? What can we offer to God and to God's people that is of value to us?

Reader 6:

Abram brought the animals to the place of sacrifice and offered them to God according to the custom of the day.

Reader 7:

God accepted the sacrifice and once again promised Abram and his descendants the land of Canaan.

Chorus:

But God did not answer Abram's question. Abram asked how he could be sure that God would do what God had promised.

Reader 7:

God sealed the promise by accepting Abram's sacrifice. Abram's sign from God was the fact that God accepted what he offered.

Reader 5:
A true relationship of trust can only exist when those involved are willing to both give and receive. What is amazing in our relationship with God is not that God gives but that God receives.

Reader 2:
God believes that we have something worth giving and God does not simply claim it.

Reader 6:
Instead, God is willing to receive what we offer as a gift.

Reader 5:
God is willing to trust us and to wait for us even after we have proved ourselves untrustworthy so many times. How can we be unwilling to wait for and trust God, who has always been trustworthy?

Reader 7:
People of faith are those who trust enough to give what they value and work for to God.

Females in Chorus:
Abram gave freely.

Males in Chorus:
God accepted Abram's gift.

Females in Chorus: A new bond was formed between God and Abram and Sarai.

Entire Chorus:
The covenant, a relationship of mutual commitment and acceptance, was established.

Reader 6:
A new bond of commitment may have been formed between Abram and Sarai and God, but Abram and Sarai did not understand the full significance of that bond.

Reader 8:
They believed that God was serious about Abram having descendants, but they weren't as certain that God had a plan for making sure that those descendants came into being. They formed a plan of their own.

Reader 7:
Sarai said to Abram:

Sarah:
You see that the LORD has prevented me from having children. Go to my slave girl, Hagar, and maybe she will bear children for me.

Reader 7:
In the culture of the time, if a woman was unable to bear a child it was her obligation to find a woman of lower social standing, usually a slave, who would bear a child for her.

Reader 6:
Abram slept with Hagar, and Abram and Hagar conceived a child. But Hagar did not consider the child to be Sarai's child; instead, she started to think of herself as better than Sarai since she was the one with a child. Abram's household was in turmoil.

Reader 8:
This was not God's plan.

Reader 6:
God intervened to restore peace to Abram's family.

Reader 7:
God spoke to Abram again, and once again promised Abram a multitude of descendants. God also promised that the covenant established with Abram would be passed on to Abram's descendants. Then God said:

God:
No longer shall your name be Abram.

Reader 8:
Which means "lofty" or "exalted."

God:
From now on your name shall be Abraham.

Reader 8:
Which means "the ancestor of multitudes."

God:
As for your wife Sarai, you shall not call her Sarai, but Sarah shall be her name. I will bless her, and moreover, I will give you a son by her. She shall give rise to nations.

Sarah:
The name Sarah means "princess."

God:
Kings of peoples shall come from her.

Sarah:
When God changed my name I knew that God's promise was for me as well as for Abraham. I knew that God's promises were for women as well as men. Both Abraham and I would have an important place in history.

Reader 6:
When God said that kings would descend from Sarah, Abraham laughed. He and Sarah were too old to have children. Wouldn't it be easier to just pass the covenant on through Ishmael, Hagar's son?

Reader 7:
But God said:

God:
Your wife, Sarah, shall bear you a son, and you shall call him Isaac. I will establish my covenant with him and with his offspring after him.

Part III

Reader 7:
Some time later, three people, sent by God, came to Abraham's tent in the middle of the afternoon, at the hottest time of the day.

Reader 6:
Abraham saw them and bowed to them in greeting.

Abraham:
Let a little water be brought, and wash your feet, and rest yourselves under the tree. Let me bring a little bread so you may refresh yourselves before you continue on.

Reader 7:
They accepted Abraham's offer. Sarah began to prepare cakes and Abraham chose a calf to prepare meat for them. Abraham brought the food to them and they ate.

Reader 6:
They asked Abraham:

Readers 1,2,4:
Where is your wife, Sarah?

Abraham:
She is there in the tent.

Reader 6:
Then one of them said,

Reader 7:
I will return to you next year, and your wife Sarah shall have a son.

Reader 6:
Sarah was listening at the tent entrance behind him. She was long past the age when women can have children; so she laughed to herself and said:

Sarah:
After I have grown old and my husband is old, shall I have pleasure?

Reader 6:
The LORD said,

God:
Why did Sarah laugh and say, 'Shall I indeed bear a child now that I am old?' Is anything too wonderful for the LORD? At the set time, in due season, Sarah shall have a son.

Reader 6:
Sarah said,

Sarah:
I did not laugh.

God:
Oh yes, you laughed.

Reader 3:
Both Abraham and Sarah heard the promise that God would give them a child. Nonetheless, they still tended to think of their own plans before they thought of God's plans.

Reader 6:
Abraham and Sarah went to live in Gerar and once again Abraham did not want anyone to know that Sarah was his wife.

Reader 7:
As they had in Egypt, Abraham and Sarah pretended to be only brother and sister. And once again a ruler...

Reader 2:
This time it was King Abimelech.

Reader 7:
...took Sarah to be his wife.

Females of the Chorus:
Poor Sarah. It happened again.

Reader 8:
If Sarah became the wife of someone other than Abraham, God's plan would not be fulfilled and the covenant would not be passed on.

Reader 5:
Perhaps one would expect God to abandon Abraham at this point and forget about the promise. After all, any reasonable person could see that Abraham was bringing disaster upon himself. But God does not abandon us even when we do stupid things.

Reader 4:
God told Abimelech that Sarah was Abraham's wife and warned him not to touch her, but to take her back to Abraham at once.
Reader 7:
Abimelech took Sarah back to Abraham. God's plan was not destroyed.
Reader 8:
Sarah and Abraham did conceive, and they had a son whom they named Isaac.
Reader 8:
The name Isaac means "he laughs."
Sarah:
God brought laughter to me when I was given a child. First I laughed in disbelief. Then I laughed in joy. Everyone who hears my story will share my laughter. Who would have thought that Abraham and I would have children? Yet we had a son in our old age.
Reader 6:
The world often laughs at people of faith and at actions taken in faith.
Reader 8:
They laugh and say that our trust in what we cannot prove is ridiculous.
Chorus:
Our ancestor was named for just such laughter.
Reader 7:
Both Abraham and Sarah laughed when God said they would have a child. They thought such a thing was impossible. Isaac's name reminds us that everything is possible for God.
Reader 6:
When Isaac was a little older, God tested Abraham.
Reader 8:
Remember, even though Abraham trusted God, he had often seemed to prefer his own plan to God's plan.
Reader 7:
God told Abraham to take Isaac into the mountains and prepare an altar to sacrifice him.
Reader 2:
Abraham did not question God. This time he did not try to find an alternative to God's plan – nor did he do anything that might disrupt God's plan.
Reader 1:
He took his son and went to the mountain and prepared the altar for sacrifice.
Reader 8:
We all know the rest of the story.
Readers 1,2,3,4,5,6,7:
An angel of the LORD called to Abraham,
God:
Do not lay your hand on the boy or do anything to him. Now I know that you fear God, since you have not withheld your son, your only son, from me.
Reader 8:
Abraham feared God the way a child fears a well-loved parent. Abraham believed that God could and would do whatever was best for Abraham and his descendants. Even when God required something difficult, Abraham trusted that God understood and saw things that Abraham could not understand or see.
Reader 7:
Abraham's willingness to give his son to God was a sign of his complete trust in God. Abraham had truly accepted his part of the covenant: all that he was and all that he had he would freely give to God.
Reader 6:
The Abraham who had been afraid and therefore said that Sarah was not his wife, the Abraham who had slept with Hagar because he thought God might need a little help in providing a son, the Abraham who had said "how will I know?"... That Abraham was finally ready to place his complete trust in God, to do what he was asked to do and leave the rest to God.
Reader 4:
Abraham's faith is revealed not only in his willingness to sacrifice his son, but also in his willingness to stop the sacrifice once he had prepared for it.
Reader 5:
At the time of Abraham, people believed that gods did demand the sacrifice of children.
Reader 3:
Abraham was not going against his culture and tradition when he took Isaac to the mountain as a sacrifice.

Reader 5:
What was unusual was to think that a god would care enough to tell an individual *not* to sacrifice his son.
Reader 4:
Abraham was willing to listen to the unusual. Abraham never stopped involving God in what he was doing. Abraham never stopped listening to God.
Reader 6:
Abraham was able to hear God's message even when he lived in a society that told him not to expect such messages. Abraham knew that God could not be bound by the norms of society.
Males of the Chorus:
As high as the heavens are above the earth, so high are God's ways above our ways and God's thoughts above our thoughts.
Females of the Chorus:
We do not know why God does what God does. But we do know that all that God does is good.
Reader 6:
Because Abraham and Sarah involved God in their lives...
Reader 7:
Because Abraham and Sarah acted on the basis of faith...
Readers 1,2,3,4,5,8:
...God blessed them and chose them as the ancestors of the one who would bring salvation to the whole world.
Reader 7:
We, too, remember Abraham and Sarah as our ancestors in faith, and we recall that God is faithful to us because of a promise first made to them.
Chorus:
My soul magnifies the Lord, and my spirit rejoices in God my Saviour.... He has helped his servant ... according to the promise he made to our ancestors, to Abraham and to his descendants forever.

The Abrahams and Sarahs of Today

Abraham and Sarah kept God at the very centre of their lives. Even when times were hard and their future seemed very unclear, they kept trusting in God and doing what they believed God wanted them to do. There are people today who follow Abraham and Sarah's example and place all of their trust in God no matter how hard things get. There are people today who are willing to leave all that is familiar because they believe that is what God wants them to do. Two such people are Agnes and James.

James' Story

My name is James. I was born in 1975 in Uganda. When I was 3 years old, my dad was arrested and executed for opposing the government. In my country children are the responsibility of the father's family; so when my dad died, his sister, who was a nun, came and took me. She knew a rich man in the town who did lots of things for charity. He agreed to take care of me. I went to live with him and his number one wife and their sons.

For a few years, I remember being happy. I had a family and a nice house and two brothers. Then the man of the family got tired of his number one wife. He had many wives and he left to live with another one. He stopped sending money and life got very hard. The woman I had called "mother" for almost five years started to take her anger out on me. She reminded me that I wasn't really her son. On bad days she would beat me or make me do very hard work.

That's when I really started praying. I prayed all the time because I knew that God was the only one who really cared about me. I prayed because I knew that I had no future in this family now that the man had stopped sending money. Praying for me was like sports. It helped me feel better and stronger.

When I was 14, things got even worse. The number of beatings increased and I was no longer allowed to go to school. I knew that I had to do something or I would soon be on the streets. I had to find my real family. I remembered my aunt who used to come to visit and who had always liked me very much. I started trying to find out where she was.

A friend of my aunt's who lived in the town told me that my aunt was in Kenya with my little sister. He told me that I needed to cross the border; then people would help me.

The problem was I didn't have a passport and I didn't have the money to bribe the right people so I could get one. If I was caught trying to cross the border without a passport, I would be arrested and beaten to death. If I didn't cross the border, I would be on the streets in Uganda with no hope and little chance of surviving.

My aunt's friend told me that I had to try and cross and I had to do it soon. He said, "Come tomorrow and I will help you." I wasn't allowed to tell anyone of my plans. I couldn't say goodbye to anyone. That night I prayed very hard that God would be with me, that I would do the right thing, and that I would have a future.

In the morning, I got up and went to the place where I was to meet my aunt's friend. While I waited for him I prayed the rosary. I didn't know all the risks that I was facing but I knew enough to be scared and to know that I had no hope but God.

My aunt's friend took me to a place near the border and introduced me to a man he had paid to smuggle me across. That man took me right up to the border gates and then told me to walk across. He wouldn't come with me. The risks were too great. What could I do? I trusted God was with me and I walked through the gate. I just pretended that I was going home. No one stopped me or asked where I was going.

When I reached the Kenya gates, I walked through and went toward the buses. My aunt recognized me because I looked like my sister. She took me to a camp where I would live. I was given a very small room with two other boys about my age. Everything was very crowded. I had no friends. I didn't speak the language well. The food was terrible. I thought things had gone from bad to worse. I prayed and prayed. Why had God taken me to such a horrible place?

After I had been there only two months, my aunt got word that she was to go to Canada. When she left, I would be alone. So there I was, not quite 15 and alone in a refugee camp. The nuns there gave me a small amount of money for myself and the two boys I lived with. I bought all our food and the oil for our stove. I cooked because they couldn't. I made sure our place was clean, and I forced myself to go to school every day.

I prayed and prayed and prayed that I would be able to go to Canada too. I prayed in all the churches I could find. I went to at least four services every Sunday. God was my only hope. Then word came that Canadian immigration would not accept me. I was too young and my aunt was not my legal guardian. My hope was shattered but still I prayed. It was that or die.

Then God worked a miracle! I was told that I could go to Canada after all! I remember how happy I was when I was sitting on the plane. At last my life would be good.

When we landed in Canada, everything was ice and freezing. I had never been so cold. I said, "God, why from all my troubles do I get more troubles?" But the more I prayed, the more I came to realize that this is the best place I could be. Here I have lots of friends. I play sports and ride my bike when the weather is good. In the winter, I ski and move all the time to keep warm. Soon I will go to university. My life is full of hope. God has been good to me!

Because unrest continues in his homeland and his aunt still has connections there, James asked that we not use his picture or his real name.

Agnes' Story

I was born in Vietnam during wartime. Just before I was born, my father was buried alive in a big grave with 20 other people because they were Catholic. My brother died in a battle and his body was never found. So many times I cried because many of my relatives suffered much.

When the Communists took over South Vietnam, my mother and I sold our possessions and bought a boat. Two days later we escaped with our friends who worked for the government. We wanted to go to Thailand or anywhere to escape. The sailor lied to us. He sailed on the ocean for two weeks and took us back to Saigon. The Communists took our friends and put them in jail. They never knew when they would be free and see their families again.

Every year we kept trying to escape again and again. We sold everything that we had to get money for living and escaping. I even quit my job (I was a secretary to the director of Minh-Duc University) because I didn't want to work for the Communists.

In March 1980, we escaped again. The priests gave us Holy Communion. We wanted to celebrate Holy Week and Easter on the ocean, but we did not succeed in our escape. The boat broke in a thunderstorm. We went back to Saigon. We tried to arrange circumstances to get away. The first month we asked to go to Hue to rebuild my father's tomb. The second and third month, we asked to go to the mountain to be farmers' helpers for my uncle. This time we lied to them. We didn't go anywhere. We hid on the roof of our friend's house. We stayed hidden there, not seeing anyone, for three months.

In June of the same year, we tried one more time. We knew this would be our last try. We would have no more gold or money to pay for any more escape attempts. We were among 132 people crowded into a narrow boat on the ocean. We were all very hungry and thirsty. The children cried and cried because we had no water to mix with the powdered milk to feed them. Pirates raped the women and robbed everything from us. They took any food and water we had. They had knives and guns. They checked our bodies and clothes, looking for diamonds and gold chains sewn under clothing. They checked on my mother. She had Our Lady's medal on her chest with the Holy Communion. The chief pirate asked her, "Are you Catholic?" She answered "yes" and he told the pirates not to touch her.

The pirates returned to attack us several times. Sometimes they had as many as four ships around our boat. They hit and kicked all the men on the boat to weaken their resistance. About half the people on the boat died. We spent three days on the ocean. By a miracle of God, we survived and eventually reached a refugee camp in Thailand. We endured still more suffering there.

On August 15, 1980, we came to Ontario, Canada. The Canadian government sponsored us. We went to school to learn English and I began to do volunteer work at a nursing home. I was thankful to God for my health and I just wanted to share with the patients in any way I could. After three months I got a job as nurse's aide.

On May 14, 1984, we became Canadian citizens. We are so grateful to the Canadian government, our dedicated teachers and all our best friends who have shared and helped us build a new life in this country. With all our heart, we thank you, Canada.

Agnes Nguyen
June 14, 1984

Doogie Dogma *(Catechism #150)*

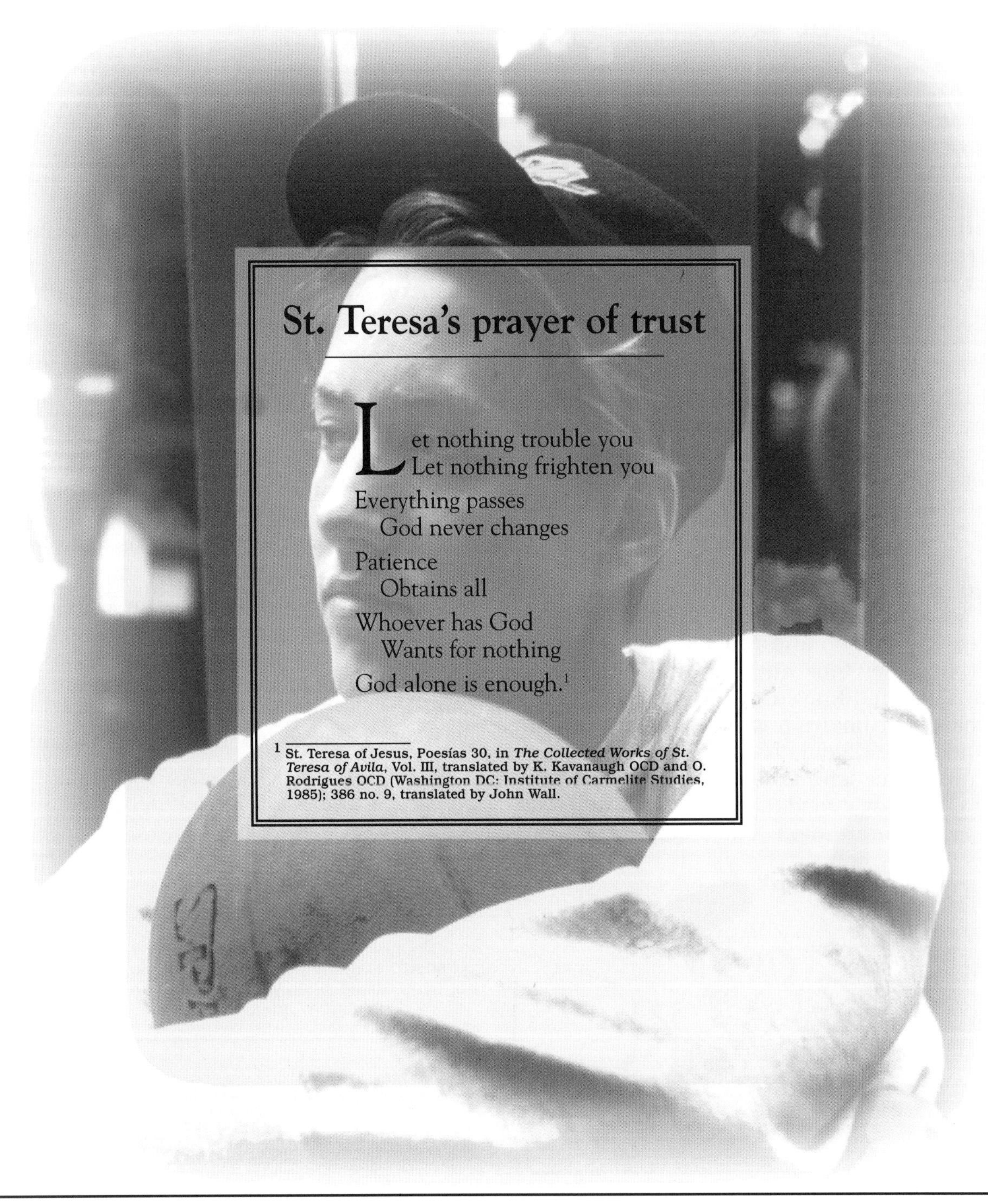

St. Teresa's prayer of trust

Let nothing trouble you
Let nothing frighten you

Everything passes
God never changes

Patience
Obtains all

Whoever has God
Wants for nothing

God alone is enough.[1]

---

1 St. Teresa of Jesus, Poesías 30, in *The Collected Works of St. Teresa of Avila*, Vol. III, translated by K. Kavanaugh OCD and O. Rodrigues OCD (Washington DC: Institute of Carmelite Studies, 1985); 386 no. 9, translated by John Wall.

2.2

Am I all on my own?

Introduction

You have spent some time looking at experiences of unexpected joy, strength and comfort in your lives. Throughout history, the Christian community has understood these experiences as signs of God's presence in our lives.

Life cannot always be explained. God cannot always be seen clearly. But stories like ours, stories of both small and big experiences of what is beyond us, help us to see a pattern. In the pattern we can come to know God.

The following story is about a man who saw the faithfulness of God in an unexpected gift of food and comfort.

The Prisoner, the Hen and the Miracles

The following is part of a true story as told by a Guatemalan Indian who was put in prison and tortured after he was falsely accused of being a guerrilla. He believed that what happened in the story was a miracle from God. He was later set free.

I was terribly hungry, yes. I would have eaten anything. And the prison guard didn't even give me a piece of tortilla. Nothing, nothing. Luckily, I could pray to God. I remembered the passage from the Acts of the Apostles, of St. Peter, of St. Paul, when they were put in prison.

Oh, that God would do something for me! That God would perform a miracle!

All this reminded me of St. Paul when he was persecuted, when he was imprisoned and how he was saved. I also remembered the passage from the Holy Bible. How did it go? Yes, you know, the man who was swallowed by a big fish. I remembered Jonah. That God saved his life when he was in the belly of a huge fish. I also felt that I was inside the belly of all those people in that military zone that I found myself inside.

I asked God to save me. It was on one night that I focused my attention a lot, a lot, a lot. And I felt that God was helping a

lot in my case. It must have been one in the morning. I had sat myself down to pray to God. It must have been an hour and a half that I remained like that praying to God. And then I felt a thing fall on top of me, and my entire body – a thing that was fresh and cool. It was like a shock, a shiver running through my whole body.

It was so soothing to me, who was dying. And I said, “Lord, my God, send any one of your children to give me something to satisfy the hunger that is gnawing at my belly!”

The next day, I prayed to God once again. It wasn't quite 10 in the morning, for sure. I looked at the small window, there on the side of the room where I was. A little window. And then I thought, yes, something was going to happen in this room. At that moment I felt something. A hen flew up and tried to rest on the edge of the window. She fell through the window, there by my side. After she had fallen, she searched for a small corner for nearly a minute and she laid an egg.

I had trouble reaching it, because my hands were chained. I had trouble. You see, the hen had approached me and laid the egg there, just beyond me. As hens must lay their eggs every 24 hours – they don't miss – she laid her egg at my feet. And the hen began to sing.

An officer came in. When she saw that he was there, the hen started to fly. She was afraid, and she started flying in every direction. The officer said: “So, you, what's happening here with that hen? If the hen lays an egg here, you better be sure to tell me because the hen belongs to the captain.”

Then he went out, closing the door. I succeeded in reaching the egg. I took the egg in my hands. The first egg laid by the hen!

The next day, at the same time, the hen came in once again. She came close to me. I petted her, that brave little hen. She laid her egg. I took it right away, while the hen was still faint, since they faint when they lay an egg. Fainting, the poor hen! Afterward, she flew quickly out the window and she sang outside.

This was a hen who gave me to eat for 16 days. That hen laid 16 eggs for me beneath my window. I felt so good! She truly helped me each time I ate one of her eggs. I always thought of God. I gave thanks to God. It is a great thing that God did for me.

Reflection questions

1. What is the miracle in this story?
2. Why does the prisoner believe that the eggs are a sign of God's presence?
3. What does this story tell us about God? about the way God provides for us?

Exodus

The Bible helps us to understand that feeding a man in prison is the kind of act that God does. Our God is a faithful God who has helped people over and over again throughout history. The pattern of God's faithfulness to the people of God begins in the Exodus.

Recall God's promise to Abraham to form from him a people. God kept this promise, and the descendants of Abraham and Sarah grew and did well.

At the beginning of the Book of Exodus, however, we see that things are not going well for Abraham and Sarah's descendants. Years earlier, during a famine, the Israelites had gone into Egypt to find work and had been made welcome. Now things had changed. The upper class of Egyptians felt threatened by these sturdy foreigners: they put slave drivers over the Israelites to make their lives hard and break their spirit. The Egyptians forced the Israelites into slavery, and made their lives unbearable with hard labour (see Exodus 1.11, 14). The Egyptians even began to drown male babies that were born to the Israelites.

When the Israelites couldn't take it anymore, they did as many oppressed peoples do – they began to rebel. But something else is very clear in their story. They cried out; God saw that they were unhappy and went to help them. (See Exodus 2.23-25.)

Through God's caring for them, a leader was raised up for them: Moses. (The early life of Moses is interesting in itself – see Exodus 2:1-22.) When the ruling pharaoh finally let the people go, Moses, with help from his brother Aaron, led the people out of the country.

The great moment of drama came as the Israelites crossed the sea. Here God's care for the people was wonderfully shown.

Soon after Pharaoh let the Israelites go, he changed his mind. He sent his army to bring them back and make them slaves again. The army chased the Israelites to the edge of the sea. When the Israelites cried out to God in fear, God rescued them. The Israelites were able to cross the Red Sea safely. Pharaoh's army was caught in it and drowned.

Forever after, the Israelites were able to thank their God, who had brought them to freedom by rescuing them and destroying their oppressors.

This is a bird's-eye view of the Exodus event, which is the central faith event for the Jewish people. (In the Bible, Exodus 1–15 contains the story from the call of Moses to the crossing of the Red Sea.)

This theme of God saving the people is one that is retold in the lives of people time after time.

The Exodus Remembered and Lived

For the Jewish people, belief in God was rooted in an understanding of all that God had done for the Israelites through the events of the Exodus. The Exodus helped the Jewish people understand that their God was "almighty." No one and nothing could stand against the one true God; anyone who really knew the Exodus story understood that. Anyone who did not really understand the Exodus story could not really understand God.

The early Christians also believed that understanding the Exodus story was an important part of understanding God. They could only see Jesus in terms of his relationship to the one almighty God who had chosen and freed the Hebrew people. When they talked about who Jesus was and the

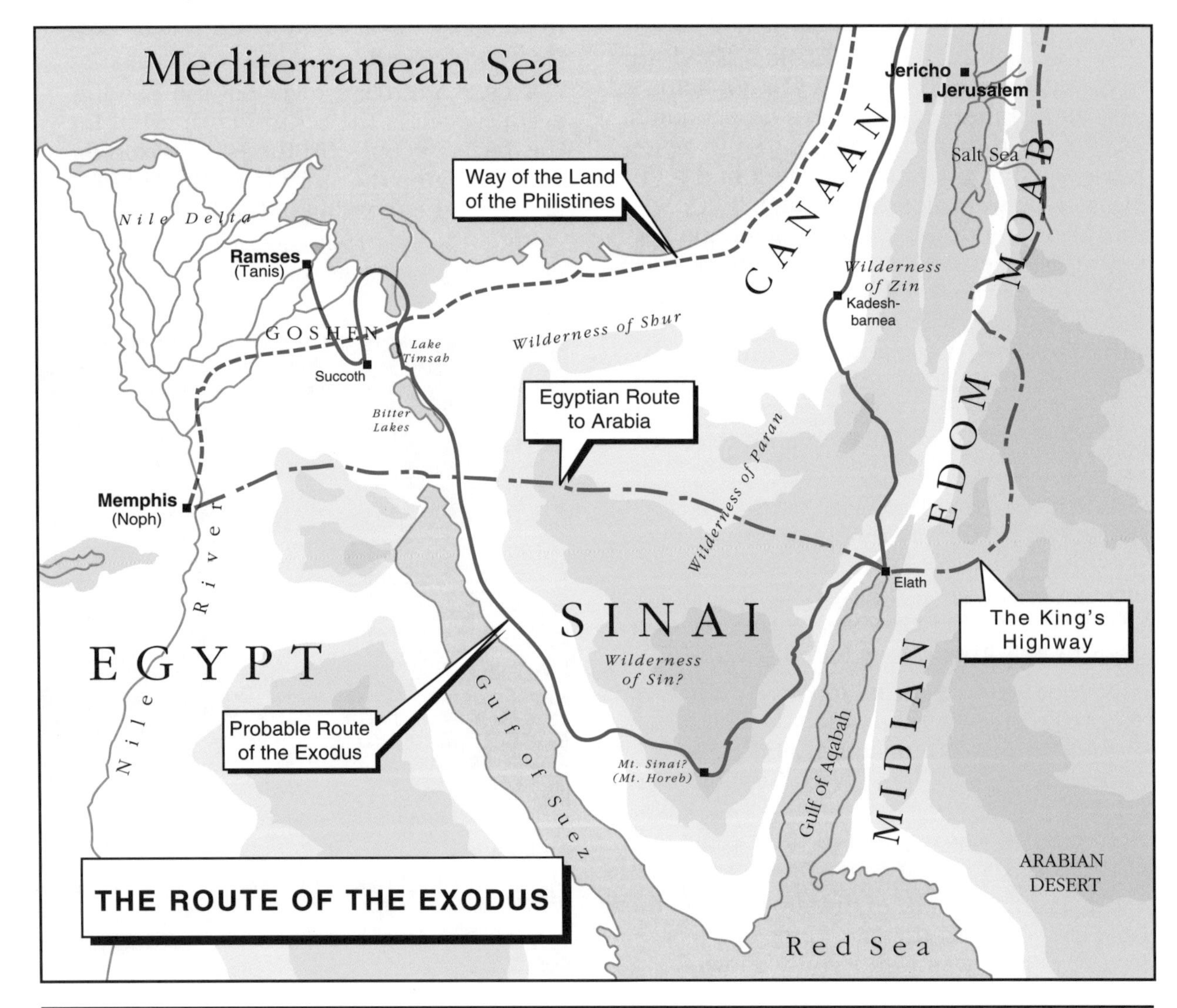

meaning of what he had done, they talked about how Jesus completed and made perfect the saving work that God had begun in the Exodus.

For both Jews and Christians, the Exodus story is central to faith. This story must be told and understood. Long before most people could read and write, special foods and rituals were used to help people remember and understand the Exodus story. These foods and rituals were part of the Passover celebration.

Just before he was crucified, Jesus went to Jerusalem with his disciples for the annual celebration of Passover. It was in the Passover meal that Jesus instituted the Eucharist. He let us know that he himself would be the food that keeps us going and the drink that gives us true hope. He reminded us that we are to share with those in need.

The Passover Meal

Jews today remember the events of the Exodus when they celebrate the Passover meal. Many of the symbolic foods that helped people understand the Exodus story in Jesus' day are still part of the Passover meal today:

- The shank bone of the lamb is the symbol of the Passover lamb. It is a reminder of the time when the Israelites marked their doorposts with the blood of a lamb as a sign of their faith in God. When the angels saw the blood, they "passed over" those houses and did not touch the Israelites' firstborn. But the firstborn of the Egyptians, who had not marked their doorposts, were killed.
- The unleavened bread symbolizes three things. First, it is the symbol of the bread of poverty that our ancestors in faith ate when they were slaves. It reminds us that God works with us when we try to bring about freedom, justice and peace. God does not abandon us, but God expects us to work with God to bring about change.

The unleavened bread also reminds us that the Israelites had very little

Prayer of Praise and Thanksgiving

All: Praise to you, O Lord our God, king of the universe, creator of the fruit of the vine, you have blessed us and given us what we need to reach this day.

Reader: The breath of all that lives shall praise you, O Lord our God. You rescue us from trouble, free us from bondage and support us through our lives. In all times of trouble and stress you show compassion. Truly we have no God but you.

All: From Egypt you rescued us, O Lord. You gave us freedom. You fed us in times of famine and sustained us in times of plenty. You taught us how to care for one another so that all might have enough. You have protected us and comforted us and given us what we need to go on living. Your loving kindness has never deserted us. Praise to you, O Lord our God, you are forever faithful.

warning when the time finally came for them to leave Egypt. This reminds us that God's timing is not our timing. We must learn to wait patiently and be prepared to act quickly when God calls.

Finally, the unleavened bread reminds us that the work of redemption that God calls us to cannot wait. There is no time to waste when justice needs to be done. In eating the unleavened bread, we commit ourselves to helping those who are treated unjustly.

- The bitter herbs remind us that Pharaoh made the lives of God's people bitter in Egypt. God does not protect us from all the bitter things in life; instead, God supports us and helps us to overcome them and even grow from them.
- The parsley dipped in salt water reminds us that faith and hope live on even through our tears and our sorrow.
- The haroset, or apple mixture, represents the mortar that the Israelites used to build Pharaoh's "treasure cities." Even when our lives are very hard, we can still do things that will make a difference in the world.

Footprints

One night I had a dream. I dreamed that I was walking along the beach with the Lord. Across the sky flashed scenes from my life. For each scene, I noticed two sets of footprints in the sand: one belonging to me, and the other to the Lord.

When the last scene of my life flashed before me, I looked back at the footprints in the sand. I noticed that many times along the path of my life there was only one set of footprints. I also noticed that this happened at the very lowest and saddest times in my life.

This really bothered me and I questioned the Lord about it. "Lord, you said that once I decided to follow you, you'd walk with me all the way. But I have noticed that during the most troublesome times in my life, there is only one set of footprints. I don't understand why when I needed you most you would leave me."

The Lord replied, "My precious, precious child, I love you and I would never leave you. During your times of trial and suffering, when you see only one set of footprints, it was then that I carried you."

Margaret Fishback Powers (adapted)

The Exodus story reminds us that without God's help, our lives would be miserable. We should always praise and thank God for the many wonderful things God has done for us. One prayer of praise and thanksgiving which we might use is the preface (introduction) to the Eucharistic Prayer of the Divine Liturgy used by the Ukranian Catholic Church.

It is right and just to sing of You, to bless You,
to praise You,
to thank You,
to worship You everywhere in Your domain;
for You are God – ineffable, inconceivable, invisible, incomprehensible, always existing and ever the same –
You and Your only-begotten Son and Your Holy Spirit.
You brought us from nothingness into being and, after we fell, You raised us again,
You did not cease doing everything until You led us up to heaven and granted us Your future kingdom.
For all these things we give thanks to You, to Your only-begotten Son and to Your Holy Spirit;
for all things which we know and do not know, the benefits bestowed upon us both manifest and hidden.[1]

[1]From the English translation of *The Sacred and Divine Liturgy of our Holy Father John Chrysostom*,

Unit 2 Summary Statements

- To say "we believe in God" is to say that we put our trust in God and we direct our lives toward God. We do not accept any substitutes for God in our lives.
- Our long faith story really begins with Abraham and Sarah. Abraham and Sarah's whole lives were shaped by their trust in God. Because Abraham trusted God even when he did not understand God's plan, he is called "our father in faith."
- To be a person who believes is to be a person who is willing to make commitments.
- God is faithful. What God says, God does.
- God kept the promise made to Abraham and Sarah. Their descendants grew and did well. During a famine they moved to Egypt, where thcy were welcomed. Centuries later, the Egyptians made them slaves. God called Moses to lead them to freedom. This event is called the Exodus.
- The story of the Exodus and of God's faithfulness to Israel is repeated over and over in the big and small events of our lives and our history. God keeps supporting us as we search. God still guides us through hard times and leads us into freedom from our many forms of slavery: for example, our whims, meanness, stupidity, peer pressure, drugs, consumerism.
- Our belief in God calls us to have patience. Without patience, it is hard to live life to the full.
- While Jesus and his disciples were celebrating the Exodus at the Passover meal on the night before he died, Jesus instituted the Eucharist.
- Jesus' death and resurrection completed and made perfect the saving work that God had begun in the Exodus.

Key Terms

Abram/Abraham	Isaac	Exodus
Sarai/Sarah	covenant	Moses
Pharaoh	trust	Passover

Unit 3

We believe in God the Father Almighty

3.1

Who loves me?

Mothers and Fathers and Love

It is hard to know how much love it takes to be a mother or father. Imagine for a moment what our parents go through for our sake.

When we were born, we did not do much more than make a lot of noise, dirty our diapers and eat a lot, often in the middle of the night. Someone had to care for us. Someone fed us, washed us and cleaned up after us. Someone held us and comforted us when we cried. Someone took time off to care for us when we were sick. Someone was patient while we were learning to walk. Someone taught us to talk. Someone showed us how to make up after a fight and how to begin again when we made a mistake.

Someone loved us even when we gave very little in return. Someone allowed his or her life to be shaped by our needs. Someone was a loving mother to us. Someone was a loving father to us. Without our parents' self-giving love, we would not be here.

If we know a parent's love, we know something about how God loves us. God's love is something like a mother's and a father's love. Like a mother or father with a young child, God loves and cares for us even when we give very little back. And as parents limit themselves when working or playing with a child, so God does with us. God is infinitely stronger, wiser and more powerful than we are, yet God does not take over or ignore our efforts. God is like a parent teaching a child how to ride a bicycle. God does not control our lives but goes along beside

"If my father and mother forsake me,
the LORD will take me up."
Psalm 27.10

"I bow my knees before the Father,
from whom every family in heaven
and on earth takes its name."
Ephesians 3.14-15

"As a mother comforts her child,
so I will comfort you;
you shall be comforted in Jerusalem."
Isaiah 66.13

us, offering encouragement and helping us keep our balance.

Yes, God loves us like a parent loves a child, but God's love goes beyond parental love. Parental love is human. It sometimes fails; it sometimes tries to control too much. God's love never fails and never takes away our freedom. God's love does not have the weaknesses and limits of human love. Even if we know that our parents loved and cared for us when we were younger, we may feel that our parents have stopped loving us. Then we can find comfort in the words of King David: Even "if my father and mother forsake me, the LORD will take me up" (Psalm 27.10).

God is the perfect parent who will always love us and will never leave us or treat us unjustly.

"Do not fear, for I have redeemed you;
I have called you by name, you are mine."
Isaiah 43.1

"Can a woman forget her nursing child,
or show no compassion for the child of
her womb?
Even these may forget,
yet I will not forget you."
Isaiah 49.15

"If you then...know how to give good gifts to your children, how much more will your Father in heaven give good things to those who ask him!"
Matthew 7.11

"Jerusalem, Jerusalem.... How often have I desired to gather your children together as a hen gathers her brood under her wings, and you were not willing!"
Luke 13.34

God is the standard for all human fatherhood and motherhood.
Catechism of the Catholic Church, #239

When No One Seems to Care: Pray

Do you ever feel like everyone, even God, has abandoned you or left you behind? Most of us feel this way at times, but it's not because God moves away from us. It's because we move away or turn away from God. We can stop feeling abandoned and lonely by turning back to God and asking for comfort. We can be sure that God will comfort us. Jesus said, "Who, if your child asks for bread, will give a stone? Or if the child asks for a fish, will give a snake? If you then…know how to give good gifts to your children, how much more will your Father in heaven give good things to those who ask him" (Matthew 7.9-11).

Think about little children calling for their mom or dad. They trust that their parents will make everything all right. Jesus tells us that when we are lonely, we can call on God in the same way. Our faith tells us that God's presence can make everything all right. If we look for God's presence in prayer, we won't be lonely anymore.

How Should We Pray?

There are many ways to pray. We can pray by simply talking with God:

- telling God what is going on in our lives
- thanking God for all the good things that have happened to us
- asking God for help with any problems we might have (some people like to imagine that God is sitting in an empty chair in the room with them when they pray like this)

We can pray by sitting quietly, watching and listening to the world that God has made. We can pray by saying the formal prayers of the Church, such as the Lord's Prayer, the Hail Mary, or the rosary. We can pray by reading the Bible and imagining that we are part of the action. We can pray by stopping during the day to share a thought with God about something around us, or to ask God to help someone we know.

There is no "right" way to pray. God will respond whenever we call out in faith and love.

God's Answers Are Not Always Our Answers: A Cautionary Tale

If you are praying and praying and getting frustrated because God does not seem to answer, think about this story:

Not far from here, there is a village that nestles in a valley where two rivers flow together.

One year, after the long winter months of snow, the weather became very warm for a few days. The rains fell and the rivers began to flood.

Most of the villagers took what they could from their homes and drove to higher ground for safety.

One man, named Credulous, refused to leave his home. His neighbours stopped on their way out of town and urged him to come with them. "I don't have to leave. I believe in God, and God will take care of me," said Credulous. "If you really had faith, you'd stay here too." But his neighbours, after trying to argue with him for a while, gave up and headed for higher ground.

By evening that day, the rivers had overflowed their banks and covered the main floor of people's houses. Firefighters came in a boat to the upstairs window of Credulous' house and urged him to get in with them and flee to safety. But Credulous still refused to leave. "The Bible says, 'Look at the birds of the air. They don't sow or reap, but God feeds them,'" said Credulous. "I know that God will take care of me."

When midnight came, the waters were deep and wild in the valley. A helicopter came for Credulous, who was now sitting on the roof of his house, but still he refused to escape. "Faith is what this world needs," he said. "If I got into your helicopter, I would be proving that I didn't believe in God."

Credulous died that night in the raging waters. When he went to heaven, he was angry with God. "I believed in you all my life," he whined. "You said that you would take care of every hair on my head. Why did you let me die?"

"But I did care for your needs, Credulous," replied the Lord. "First, I sent your neighbours to urge you to leave your home. Then I sent the firefighters in their boat, and finally I sent the helicopter to save your life. Why did you reject all my efforts to save you?"

3.2

It's a "free country." Why shouldn't I do whatever I want ?

My Friend[1]

Malik, son of Dinar, was very upset about how a youth who lived next door was acting. For a long time, Malik did nothing, hoping that someone else would. But when the youth's behaviour became really bad, Malik went to him and told him to change his ways.

The youth calmly replied that he was protected by the ruler of the country and so nobody could stop him from living however he wanted to live.

Malik said, "I shall personally complain to the ruler."

The youth replied, "That will be quite useless. He will never change his mind about me."

"I shall denounce you to God," Malik said.

"God is far too forgiving to condemn me," the youth said.

Malik went away knowing he had failed. But after a while, the youth's reputation became so bad that there was a public outcry about it. Malik decided that it was his duty to try to scold him. As he was walking to the youth's house, however, he heard a voice say to him, "Do not touch my friend. He is under my protection." Malik was very confused by this and, when he was in the presence of the youth, did not know what to say.

The young man asked, "What have you come for now?"

"I came to scold you," Malik said, "but on my way here a voice told me not to touch you, for you are under his protection."

The youth seemed stunned. "Did the voice call me 'friend'?" he asked. But by then, Malik had already left his house. Years later, Malik met this same man at a holy site. The youth had been so touched by the words of the voice that he had given up everything he owned and had gone to serve the poor. "I have come here in search of my Friend," he said to Malik.

[1] From Anthony de Mello, *The Song of the Bird.* Toronto: Doubleday, 1982. (slighty adapted)

Reflection questions

1. Why did the youth refuse to listen to Malik when Malik first complained about his behaviour?
2. Why did the voice affect the youth so much?
3. Why did the youth decide to give up everything and serve the poor?

Think About This:

God loves us and is faithful to us no matter what we do. That means that everything we do matters. If we accept God's love for us, we will *want* to live lives of love and to make a difference in the world. Because God loves us, we will be *able* to live lives of love and to make a difference in the world.

Directions for "Boxes of Respect"

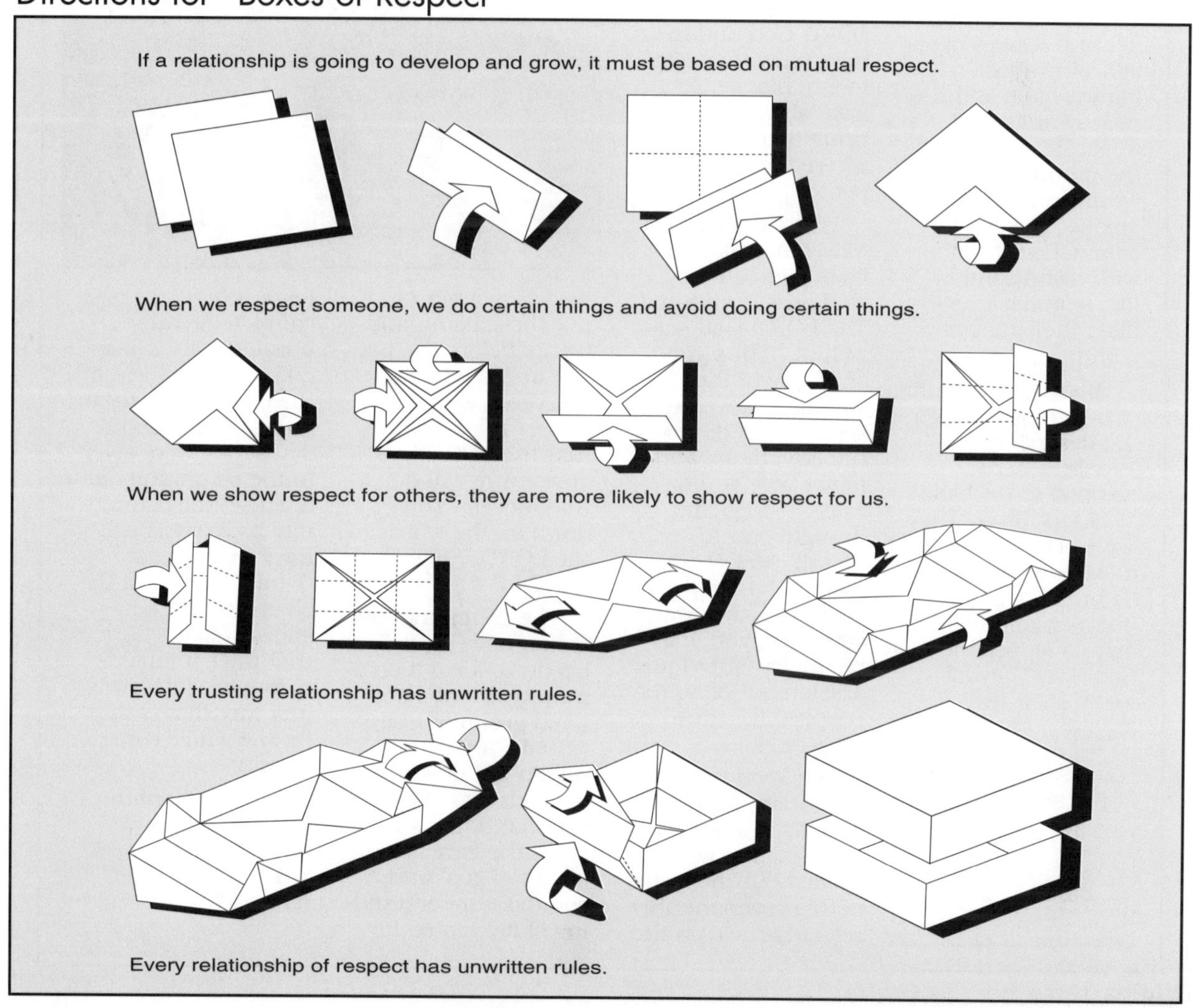

The Mountain and Desert Gazette

Earthshaking event at Mount Sinai

Sinai

Great peals of thunder and flashes of lightning shook Mount Sinai and the nearby areas last week. Witnesses saw the mountain wrapped in thick smoke. The great commotion, together with awful sounds like trumpet blasts, filled the Israelites with fear.

After three months of travelling through the desert, the Israelites were camped at the base of Mount Sinai. They have been on the move ever since they fled the Egyptian pharaoh and his armies across the Red Sea. They followed their leader, Moses, who claims to have spoken with the LORD God and to have a divine mission to free his people from slavery and to bring them to a land where they can prosper.

It is reported that Moses has again been contacted by God on Mount Sinai. The LORD God said to him, "Thus you shall say to the... Israelites: You have seen what I did to the Egyptians, and how I bore you on eagles' wings and brought you to myself. Now therefore, if you obey my voice and keep my covenant, you shall be my treasured possession out of all the peoples" (Exodus 19.3-5).

While on the mountain, Moses was given Ten Commandments, which spelled out the terms of this covenant. (See related article on the next page.) Moses put these commandments before the people, and the Israelites answered with one voice: "'All the words that the LORD has spoken we will do.' And Moses wrote down all the words of the LORD." (See Exodus 24.3-4.)

The commandments have already begun to form a community out of a scattered group of individuals, a great nation out of a band of ex-slaves. The commandments have given the Israelites a common goal and a common understanding of life rooted in respect. Even so, the camp is already buzzing with talk as different members of the community try to interpret them. But since they were given to the community as a whole, the community as a whole will have to interpret them. Moses and the elders have taken steps to make sure that the commandments are interpreted in a way that is best for the whole community.

In the meantime, the smoke has cleared from Mount Sinai. At least...for now.

Ten Steps to the Good Life

Tired of empty promises? We have God's own word that anyone who follows these Ten Steps to the Good Life will indeed have the "good life." And here's the best news of all – you get to the good life just by trying your best to follow these Ten Steps, or commandments. You will get results even the very first day! You don't have to wait a lifetime to find the good life.

Those who believe that the "good life" includes freedom are right. Although these commandments seem to limit our freedom, they actually give us more freedom. Finding true freedom includes developing good relationships. We're only free if our relationships are rooted in respect. Without respect, neither love nor friendship is possible.

Relationships built on respect make us truly free and happy.

Here are the Ten Commandments:[2]

1. I am the LORD your God who brought you out of slavery. You shall not have other gods besides me.
2. You shall not misuse the name of the LORD your God.
3. Remember the sabbath day, and keep it holy.
4. Honour your father and mother.
5. You shall not kill.
6. You shall not commit adultery.
7. You shall not steal.
8. You shall not bear false witness against your neighbour.
9. You shall not covet your neighbour's spouse.
10. You shall not covet anything that belongs to your neighbour.

[2] See Exodus 20.1-17.

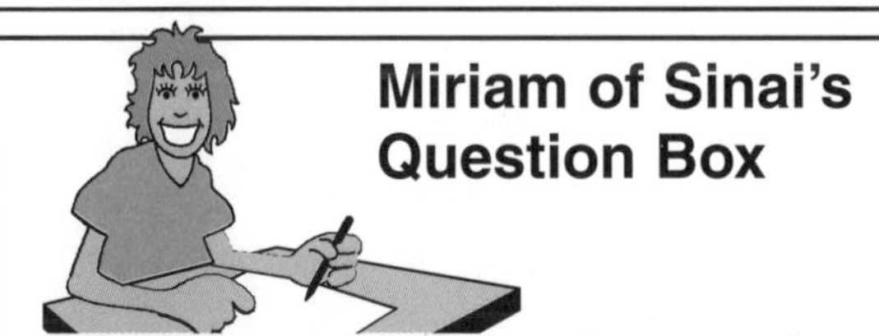

Miriam of Sinai's Question Box

Q Dear Miriam,
I was a slave for most of my life, building pyramids and palaces for the Egyptian pharaohs. When Moses promised us slaves our freedom, we followed him. Next thing you know, we're wandering in the desert, barely scraping by. At least in Egypt we always knew where our next meal would come from. Now we have to hope for strange bread from the sky and water from rocks. Every day we're afraid. How could you call this freedom?

Now let me ask you, do *you* know where and how to find true freedom?
Signed,

Bamboozled in Meribah

A Dear Bamboozled,
You say that Moses has taken you from bad to worse, but the truth is Moses has made it possible for you to find true freedom. Without Moses, you would never have gone to Mount Sinai and heard the voice of the one true God. Only God can give true freedom. If you look to anyone or anything else to give you lasting freedom and happiness, you won't find it. You cer-

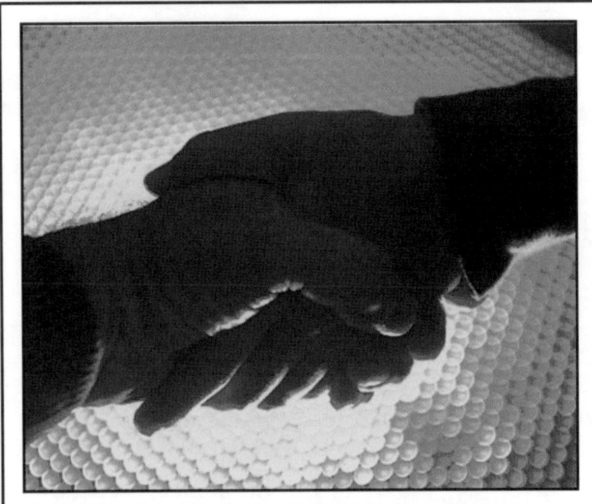

If you want freedom, respect God and God's authority.

tainly wouldn't have found freedom in Egypt where Pharaoh tried to muffle the voice of God.

A good place to start your search for true freedom is to listen carefully to the words God has spoken. Begin with the first three commandments of the Ten Commandments. Each of these commandments tells you what to do to remain truly free.

The first commandment says, "I am the LORD your God, who brought you out of...slavery. You shall have no other gods besides me." Many things and people try to make us into something we were never meant to be. Only God allows us to become the best people we can be. If you want freedom, respect God and God's authority. Do not follow people who would deny God's power or try to make God's power their own. Show respect for God, and do not act as if you didn't need God.

Number two: "You shall not misuse the name of the LORD your God." You may think that this commandment limits your freedom of speech. The truth is, the commandment reminds us how important speech is and how it can lead us away from freedom if we use it unwisely.

When we misuse God's name, we are misusing the power of communication. When it becomes a habit, it results in unhealthy or broken relationships. Unhealthy and broken relationships prevent us from developing our potential. They keep us from being free.

Three: "Remember the sabbath day, and keep it holy." If you want to be free, you must stop regularly to look at your life and your relationship with God and others. If you don't do this, you can start some bad habits. If you do not put God first, you might not be able to resist those things or people that are trying to control you. The Sabbath is a day when we celebrate the freedom God gives us and when we recommit ourselves to showing respect for God and other people.

Q Dear Miriam,
I was so excited when we left Egypt and set out on the road to freedom. I thought that travelling in a large group would

Brain Teasers

Here are four coded commandments. Can you figure out what they are?

1. ❙❏◆ ▲❈❁●● ■❏▼ ❈❁❖❅ ❏▼❈❅❒ ❇❏❄▲ ❂❅▲❉❄❅▲ ❍❅
2. ❈❏■❏◆❒ ❙❏◆❒ ❆❁▼❈❅❒ ❁■❄ ❍❏▼❈❅❒
3. ❙❏◆ ▲❈❁●● ■❏▼ ❂❅❁❒ ❆❁●▲❅ ◗❉▼■❅▲▲
4. ❙❏◆ ▲❈❁●● ■❏▼ ❃❏❖❅▼

give me a chance to get away from my parents. I was planning on hanging out with the family of one of my friends. My family really limits my freedom – since Moses was calling us to freedom I thought for sure he'd support my decision. But now people are telling me that I'm forgetting the fourth commandment. What is it and what does it have to do with freedom?

Signed,

Longing for independence

A Dear Longing,
The fourth commandment is "Honour your father and mother." We can find freedom when we accept and respect the families God has given us. We cannot be free if we spend our time wishing that we had been given a different family. If we work on building healthy relationships rooted in respect within our families, we will find it easier to develop healthy and freeing relationships outside of our families.

Q Dear Miriam,
My best friend and I had a fight a year ago. I felt so angry with her that I did everything I could to get even for what happened. Now I feel sad that our friendship has been broken. What advice can you give on developing healthy and freeing relationships?

Signed,

Forlorn

A Dear Forlorn,
Respect yourself and those around you. In everything you do, remember that true friendship is rooted in respect. If we respect others, we will not wish them harm. We will not treat them as objects. We will not try to hurt their reputation or take what belongs to them. We will not wish to destroy relationships that are important to them. If we respect ourselves, we will not think that we need what someone else has to be happy or to be a valuable person.

Respect yourself and others – follow the 5th, 6th, 7th, 8th, 9th and 10th commandments – and you will again be able to develop healthy, lasting and freeing relationships.

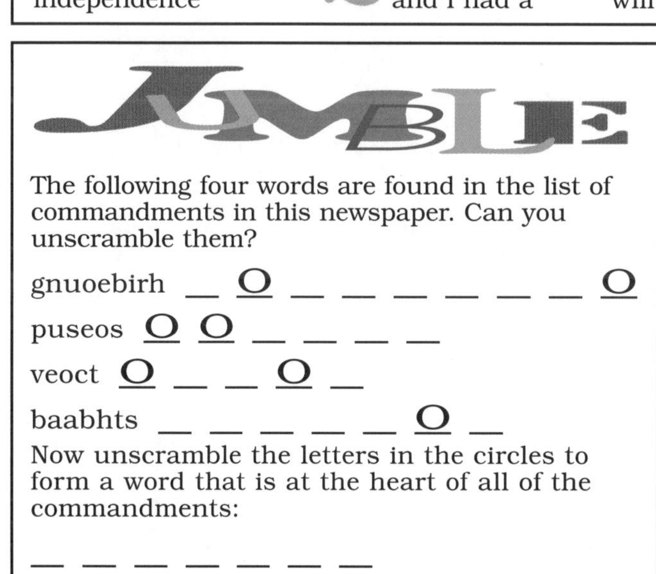

JUMBLE

The following four words are found in the list of commandments in this newspaper. Can you unscramble them?

gnuoebirh _ O _ _ _ _ _ _ _ O

puseos O O _ _ _ _

veoct O _ _ O _

baabhts _ _ _ _ _ O _

Now unscramble the letters in the circles to form a word that is at the heart of all of the commandments:

_ _ _ _ _ _ _

S P O R T S

The Match Is On!

It's the match-up of the century! At last we will see who are the overall winners in the great contest of life. The contestants are the Coveters and the Covenantors.

For centuries, the Coveters have said they are better. They say that the only way to get ahead is to take whatever you can. If someone has something that you need and you can get it, "go for it." According to the Coveters, people who worry about breaking relationships get broken by relationships.

The Covenantors believe that, in the long run, the Coveters will always lose: "They may be faster in the short distances, but they have no endurance." According to the Covenantors, you will have a better life if you are willing to limit yourself sometimes in order to develop strong, supportive friendships. They claim that if we are faithful to others even when it doesn't seem to help us, we will enjoy life more. When we need help, others will come to our aid even when we have nothing to give in return. The Covenantors say that possessions will not make us happy if we have no one to enjoy them with.

The contest is life. The goal is true freedom. The Covenantors have accepted the Sinai covenant and the commandments from God. They will try to find freedom and happiness in relationships built on love and respect.

The Coveters have rejected the commandments. They are out for whatever they can get and whatever feels good at the moment. They will try to find freedom and happiness in getting as much as they can.

For those of you who have not been following the story behind this match-up, we would like to remind you that "to covet" means to want something that

belongs to someone else so much that you wish to take it away from the other person and keep it for yourself. If you covet something, in your heart you are stealing what God has allowed another person to have. If you covet a person, in your heart you are breaking a relationship that has been made by God. To covet something is to wish that another person would suffer for our benefit. To covet is to ignore the command to love.

A covenant is a commitment based on a promise. It is guaranteed only by the good word of the individuals who make it. When people enter into a covenant, they agree to limit their individual behaviour in order to develop that covenant relationship. Each person agrees that when it comes to making decisions, what is good for the relationship will be more important than what is good for him or her as an individual. When two people pledge their friendship to one another, they make a covenant. Friends help friends who are in need even if they would rather be doing something else.

The stakes are high. Who are you betting on?

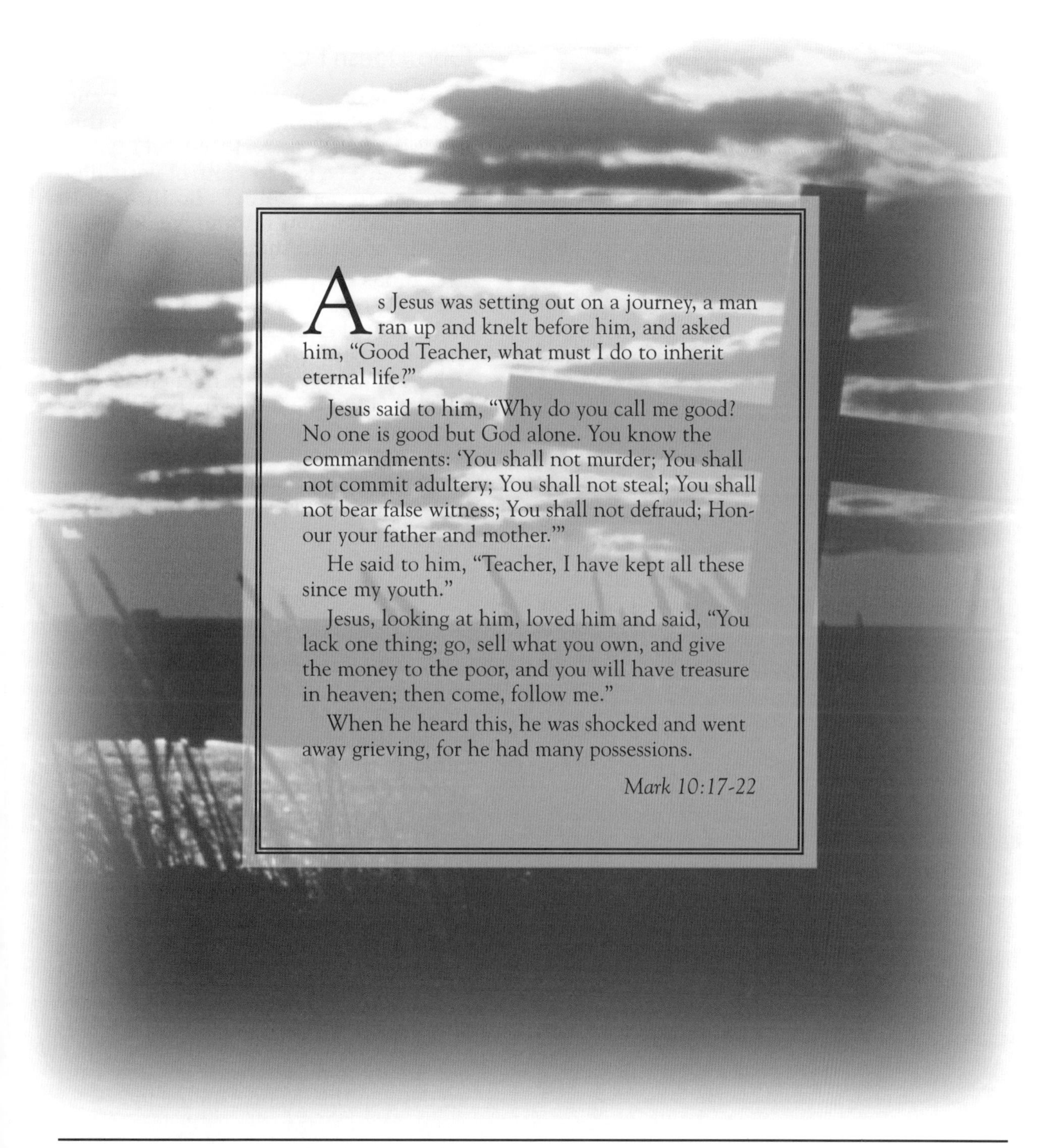

As Jesus was setting out on a journey, a man ran up and knelt before him, and asked him, "Good Teacher, what must I do to inherit eternal life?"

Jesus said to him, "Why do you call me good? No one is good but God alone. You know the commandments: 'You shall not murder; You shall not commit adultery; You shall not steal; You shall not bear false witness; You shall not defraud; Honour your father and mother.'"

He said to him, "Teacher, I have kept all these since my youth."

Jesus, looking at him, loved him and said, "You lack one thing; go, sell what you own, and give the money to the poor, and you will have treasure in heaven; then come, follow me."

When he heard this, he was shocked and went away grieving, for he had many possessions.

Mark 10:17-22

3.3 Who's in control?

God Doesn't Control Us

Does it ever seem like too many people are trying to make you do things their way? Do you ever feel that even your friends are trying to control your life? Wanting to make others do things our way is a common human weakness. If we can control others, most of us do it.

God has the power to make us obey, but God chooses not to use that power. Instead, God gives us the ability to see the difference between good and bad, between right and wrong, and then lets us decide what to do. In the words of the prophet Jeremiah (see Jeremiah 31.33), God places God's own law within us and writes it upon our hearts. God then gives us the freedom to accept or reject that law. The choice between love and sin is ours.

When we reject God's law and choose sin, we hurt God's creation. Yet God loves us so much that the freedom to choose – even to choose sin – is still ours. This freedom to make sinful choices gives our loving choices value. If we could not make sinful choices, we would not be able to make truly loving choices, either. If the only words we could say were "I love you," would it mean very much when we told someone that we loved him or her? If the only choices we could make were loving choices, what would an act of love really mean?

God teaches us how to choose wisely while giving us the freedom to make our own choices and to grow in our own way. Our all-powerful God allows us to decide what will happen to us and to creation. Do we understand what an incredible gift our ability to decide really is? How can we develop this wonderful ability?

How to Make Good Decisions

When you have to make an important decision, here are some questions to ask yourself:

Step	Meaning	Questions to ask yourself
1. OBSERVE	Look carefully at what is involved in the situation. Investigate!	• How could someone be helped in this situation? • How could someone be hurt in this situation? • How did this situation come about? • Is there more to the story? • What options are available? • What effect will the decision have on the person who makes it? • Who else will be affected by this decision? How?
2. JUDGE *[Assess and Choose]*	Consider what is the right decision. Evaluate!	• What are the pros and cons of each option? • What commandment of God, teaching of Jesus or teaching of the Church tells me what is the right thing to do? • What is the opinion of those with experience? • Have I made similar decisions in the past? What happened? • Have I prayed about this? • Be honest: is it really right or wrong? • What is the *best* decision I can make in this situation?
3. ACT	Do what is right.	• What help do I need so that I will do what is truly best? • What do I need to do now?
4. RE-EVALUATE	Re-examine what you've done.	• Would I do this again? • Do I need to do something else now?

In every decision we make, we must remember three basic rules:

1. Evil may never be done to bring about a good result. (A decision to do evil is always immoral even if the end result is good.)
2. In everything, we should show the same care for others that we want them to show for us.
3. In every decision, we must respect the consciences of those around us. We must never do anything that would make it harder for others to tell right from wrong.

Once we know the best thing we can do, then we know the "right thing to do," and therefore we know what God is asking us to do.

Hard Choices

The "right" thing to do is not always the easiest thing to do. Yet we believe that God sees the good that we do and rewards it in unexpected ways. The Bible is full of stories of people who made hard choices because they knew that those choices were "right." These choices to do good often made life hard in the short run, but they brought blessings in the long run.

Think about the story of the widow of Zarephath (see 1 Kings 17.8-24). The widow shared the very last of her food with the prophet Elijah, even though she believed that she and her son would soon starve to death. God saw how giving she was and rewarded her for it. The small amount of food that she had left would last for another day. The next day, the widow once again shared the last of her food with Elijah. Once again, God rewarded her with enough for another day. And so it went. The widow shared, day after day, never knowing if the food would run out. The food lasted until the drought ended. Because the widow fed

Elijah day after day, Elijah was there when her child got very sick and stopped breathing. Elijah called out to God and reminded God of the widow's generosity and faith. God listened to Elijah and agreed that the widow's willingness to do what was right even when it was risky should be rewarded. The child lived.

God is the perfect parent who wants what is best for us. Although God may ask us to do things that we find hard, God never asks us to do anything that will hurt us in the long run. God's ways do not always make sense to us because God sees a much bigger picture of the world than we do. If we follow the guidelines that God has given us and listen to the law of God that is written on our hearts, we will find true happiness and freedom. If we think only of ourselves and of what we want right now, we will find loneliness, insecurity and frustration. The choice is ours.

Doogie Dogma *(Catechism #1791)*

"I will put my law within them, and I will write it on their hearts; and I will be their God, and they shall be my people."
Jeremiah 31.33

Unit 3 Summary Statements

- When we say that we believe in "God the Father Almighty," we are saying that
  - God's love, tenderness, compassion and forgiveness are a model for all human parents.
  - God is an almighty parent. Although human parents may fail their children, God will never fail.
  - We are all children of one God; therefore, we are all brothers and sisters.
- Just as parents give young children rules to keep them safe, so God gives us rules to keep us safe from sin.
- The Ten Commandments call us to live a life that is rooted in respect for God, for others and for ourselves.
- God loves us so much that God has made a covenant with us. We accept the covenant by obeying the commandments.
- Although God could control us, God does not. God gives each one of us the freedom to choose and to find our own way to union with God.
- Each person is responsible for developing and using his or her conscience.
- When you have to make a major decision, follow these steps: observe, judge, act.
- Three rules apply in every situation:
  - Choosing to do evil in order to bring about a good result is an immoral (wrong) choice.
  - We should always show the same care for others that we want them to show us.
  - We must respect the consciences of others.

Key Terms

God: the perfect parent
prayer
love
respect
Ten Commandments
freedom
covet
covenant
decision making:
observe, judge, act, re-evaluate
sin

Unit 4

We believe in God...
the Creator of heaven and earth

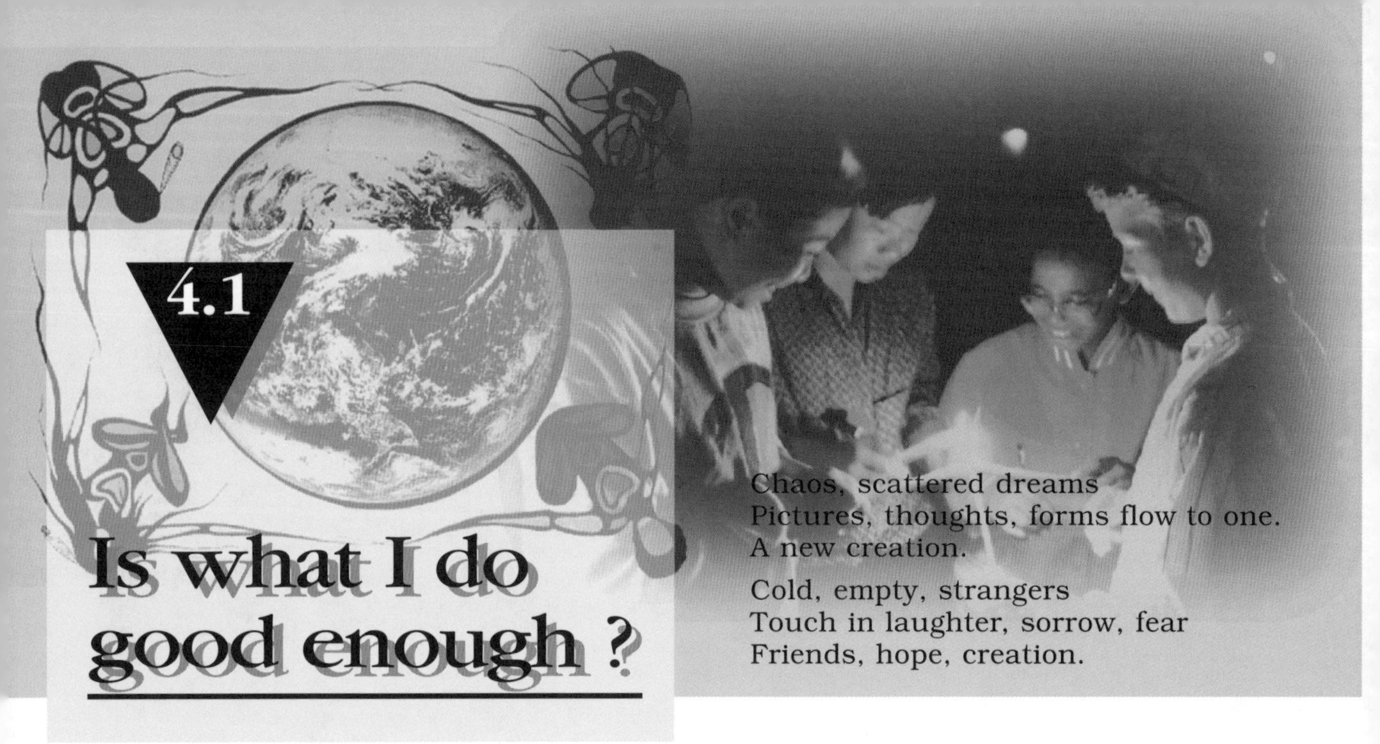

4.1 Is what I do good enough ?

Chaos, scattered dreams
Pictures, thoughts, forms flow to one.
A new creation.

Cold, empty, strangers
Touch in laughter, sorrow, fear
Friends, hope, creation.

The Creative You

You are a creative person. You give shape to the world. You put together thoughts and images in ways that are unique to you. You build relationships that no one else can copy. You bring together ideas, things and people that have never been together before. You join them to make something totally new. Without your creativity, the world would not be the same.

Humans are creative because we are made in the image of God, who is the creator of everything. God created a universe that is always changing and becoming something new. Human beings help shape what God's creation is becoming. We can co-operate with God by loving and helping complete the work of creation, or we can refuse to co-operate with God by rejecting love and hurting creation.

Creativity: Developing a Balanced Relationship with the Environment

The story of Adam and Eve, found in chapters 2 and 3 of Genesis, helps us to understand what it means to work with God in creation. In this story, God creates trees and all other vegetation only after creating a human person to care for them. It was God's plan that people would take care of the environment. In return, nature would provide the things that people needed to live. People were to have a balanced relationship with the earth. They were not to take more than they needed.

God tells Adam not to eat the fruit from the tree of the knowledge of good and evil. The fruit of this tree is the power to ignore the wants and needs of others. It represents the power to destroy. When individuals or communities believe that they can completely understand and control everything, they begin to think of themselves as gods. When they believe that they have a right to hand out good and evil as they wish, they begin to act as if they were gods. We are not gods. We cannot survive if we try to act as though we were gods.

This story of Adam and Eve reminds us that human beings are capable of using what we find in nature to control rather than love others. We see the truth of the story all around us. Many of us buy luxury goods while others go hungry and homeless. Harmful agricultural practices that seek to maximize profits can cause long-term damage to the environment and to the health of agricultural workers. Certain types of logging result in a lot of wood and a high profit but can destroy the forests for generations to come. On the east coast of North America, so much cod was taken that now the fisheries are closed. The list goes on. We sometimes use nature, taking the good things for us and using the evil things to harm others. Adam – and all humanity – is warned that misusing nature to get power for ourselves will bring death to creation.

Do you use the gifts of nature in a way that is good for all people? Is your relationship with the environment creative or destructive?

Creativity: Accepting Responsibility for the Natural World

God does not want us to abuse creation. God does not expect us to leave everything exactly the way we find it, either. In the Genesis story, God invites Adam to name each animal. In the Bible, the power to name something meant giving shape and direction to it – starting a relationship with it. The invitation to name what God creates is an invitation to help shape creation. In accepting the invitation to name the animals, Adam accepts humanity's responsibility for the natural world. Adam, and all humankind, also gets the right to use what is found in the natural world – plants, animals, water, etc. – so that people can survive.

Do you do what you can to take care of the environment? Do you do what you can to improve the environment?

Creativity: Developing Positive Relationships with One Another

God works with Adam to create Adam's partner. God says that it is not good for Adam to be alone, and so God creates all of the different animals and brings them

to Adam. Adam names them but does not find one that would be a good partner for him. Not one of the animals could be Adam's equal in shaping and directing creation. (How would you imagine the conversation between God and Adam as God brings each animal to Adam and Adam watches in vain for a partner?)

Finally, when Adam is asleep, God forms another human being from Adam's own body. (How do you think Adam felt knowing that God used Adam's very self for creation?) Adam not only gives a name to this new human being, Adam also renames himself. Adam's old name was "human being." Adam's new name is "man" and the new human is "woman." The relationship of their names (in Hebrew) shows that they are to be partners for each other.

The man and the woman are equals. Each will influence and help the other to become the best person he or she can be. The man and the woman will grow and change as they love one another. Their relationship will be something new in creation. Together they will bring new life to the world – not only in the children that they will have, but also in the way they will change one another, and in the way that their relationship to each other will change the world. As they build their relationship, they will be sharing with God in the ongoing creation of the world.

Do you treat other people as your equals or do you look down on some people? Do the ways you relate with others give new happiness, love and hope to the world?

O LORD, our Sovereign,
how majestic is your name in all the earth!

You have set your glory above the heavens.
Out of the mouths of babes and infants you have
founded a bulwark
because of your foes,
to silence the enemy and the avenger.

When I look at your heavens, the work of your
fingers,
the moon and the stars that you have established;
what are human beings that you are mindful of them,
mortals that you care for them?

Yet you have made them a little lower than God,
and crowned them with glory and honour.
You have given them dominion over the works of
your hands;
you have put all things under their feet,

all sheep and oxen, and also the beasts of the field,
the birds of the air, and the fish of the sea,
whatever passes along the paths of the seas.

O LORD, our Sovereign,
how majestic is your name in all the earth!

Psalm 8

4.2 That's not my job! Is it ?

Genesis: Beginnings

Have you ever wondered how our universe began, and how it continues to unfold in such beautiful balance and harmony? Why are the seasons so regular? How do those Canada geese know where to fly as the seasons change? How do our bodies heal when they are hurt? Together with scientists, artists and poets we stand in awe as, day after day, we witness creation.

Long before Jesus lived on this earth, the Israelites told stories of creation. We find these stories in the Book of Genesis, which means "beginnings." Genesis is not only the first book of the Bible; it is also the beginning of our own story. It is the story of who we are.

The author of the creation story draws a "word picture" about God and creation. The storyteller is like an artist who paints with words. Can you picture in your mind what this ancient storyteller is saying?

Read the first story of creation in Genesis 1.1–2.4.

1. If you had to draw a picture of God based on this story, what would God look like?
2. What does God create?
3. How does God create?
4. How is God's "making" different from all other making?
5. People see creation in many ways: some see it as good, others see it as evil, and some see it as neither good nor evil. How does God see what was created?
6. God gave us the world and asked us to care for it. What are some ways each of us must care for creation?

Two Creation Stories

The creation story found in Chapter 1 of Genesis was written around the year 500 BCE – about 500 years *after* the story in Chapter 2. Each story was written to help us understand a different part of the truth about God. Both stories are important. Both stories tell us something about God and about ourselves. Neither story tells us all there is to know about creation.

The author of the older creation story, the one in Chapter 2, stresses that God is very near, and that God wants to share in all that is going on in our lives. The author of the creation story in Chapter 1 wants to make it clear that God is also all powerful. Even though God works with human beings, God has a plan that goes far beyond what human beings can understand. The author of Chapter 1 also stresses that God has created a universe that is well ordered. Human beings must honour the balance in the universe if they are going to do the job God has given them: taking care of the earth.

Both creation stories tell us that there is only one God; God made the whole world; all that God made is good; and God creates out of love for people. Both stories also make it clear that woman and man are equal to each other, and they are "put in charge" of creation.

If it seems strange to you that there are two different creation stories, think about some event, such as a party, that you and your friends were at together. When you talk about it, you do not all remember it in exactly the same way. The stories you share are different. Even your version of the story may change when you talk with different people. Although the stories may be quite different, all of them may still be true. They may just be focusing on different parts of the truth. All of us tell things in different ways, depending on our personalities and on who we are talking to. The same may be said of the people who wrote the stories in the Bible.

Science Describes Beginnings

The storytellers who gave us the first and second creation stories in the Bible were not scientists. They were not trying to teach a science lesson about the beginnings of this planet and of humanity. They wanted to tell us something else. We can see that the details in Genesis 1 and Genesis 2 are not the same, but both stories agree that there is one loving God who created the universe. The Bible is a story of God and God's people. These storytellers begin this story of God for us.

If we want the story from a scientific viewpoint, we ask scientists. Scientists can tell us about how this universe developed since a point in time. They can tell us how many billions of years ago the earth was a blob of molten rock. It took a long time to cool off before oceans appeared. Millions of years later, creatures developed in the oceans and later on the land as well. For a time, dinosaurs lived on the earth. Relatively speaking, humans appeared only recently. (See the time line diagram on the next page for more information.)

How do we know these things? How can scientists be so sure about these facts? Do a little reading on the subject. Learn about geological formations, fossils, archeological evidence, and what all these can tell us about the past. You will find that science has valuable things to tell us. Albert Einstein once said, "Science without religion is lame; religion without science is blind." What do you think he meant?

“Science without religion is lame; religion without science is blind.” Albert Einstein

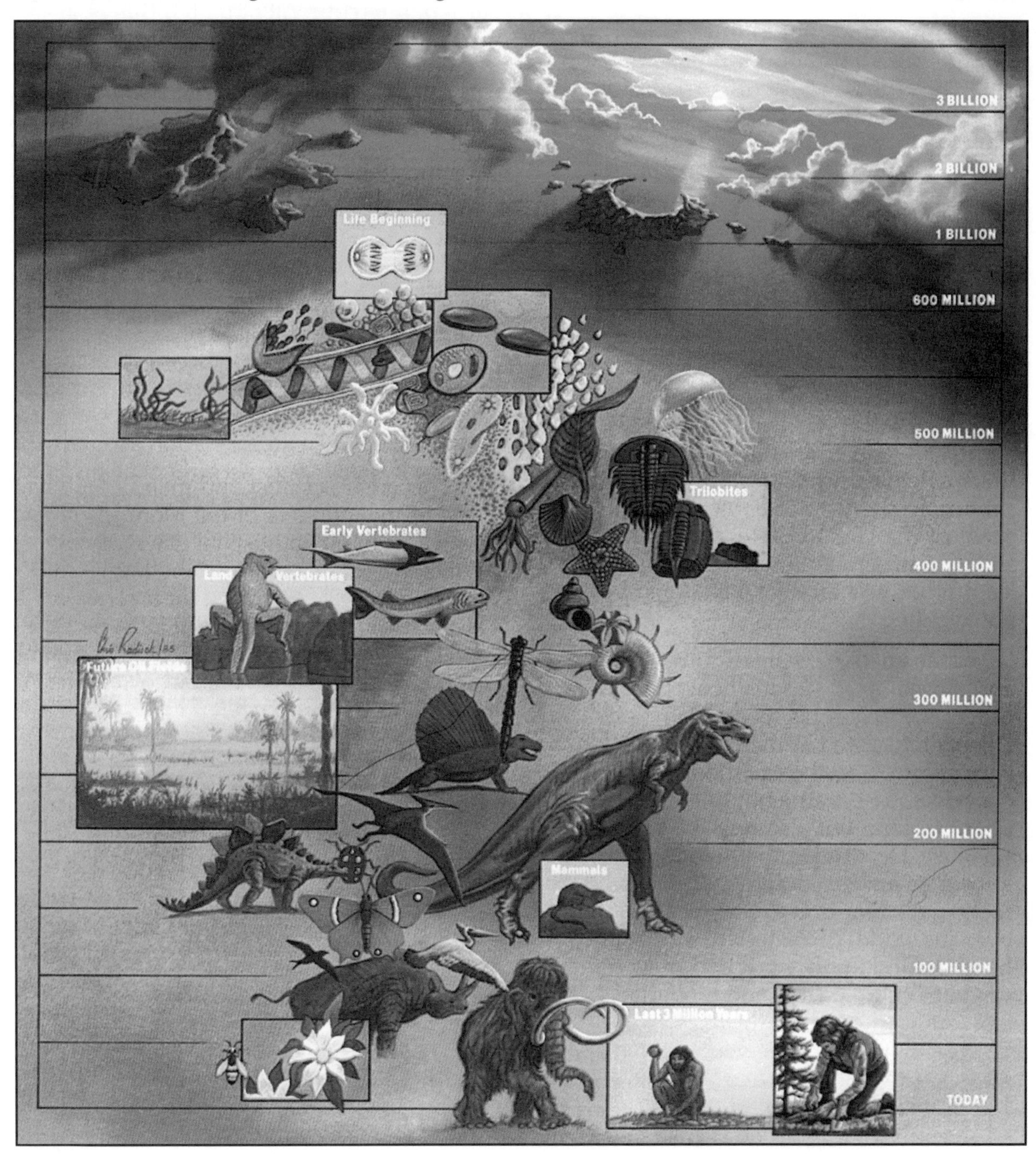

Sister Mac: One Who Cared for Creation

A train whistle hooted as she pressed the final shovelful of dirt around the roots of the young tree. This was a strange place and time for a nun to plant a tree, and the hooting train whistle seemed to echo my feelings exactly. You see, in a matter of months this spot was to be paved over, along with my home and my grandparents' home down the block. If you know Winnipeg, there is a huge railway yard in the middle of the city, just a few blocks from where I live. It's an interesting part of town, to say the least. Mostly poor working folks and lots of kids. My buddies and I enjoyed meeting the transients who would ride into town on the freight trains. They always had fantastic stories to tell, even though we didn't believe most of them. My folks didn't think much of our hanging around with these guys. Anyway, in a few months, bulldozers were to clear the area for a huge bridge to carry traffic over the railway yard. My family didn't want to move. We liked our neighbourhood. Besides, where would we go? We couldn't afford to move. But other people in the city wanted a bridge so that they could get to where they were going more quickly.

However, there was this nun. Her name was Sister Geraldine MacNamara, but we all called her Sister Mac. She lived just down the street. Sister Mac kept getting in the way of the city planners. One day she organized us to demonstrate. Another day she led us to City Hall where we had a sit-in. We signed petitions. And then there she was planting trees! I thought she was crazy.

We were just a small group of people living in a poor part of town, and we were up against the city, which wanted to improve the traffic flow. Progress, right? Maybe for those who would be using the bridge, but we were losing our homes! This was not just! Finally, Sister Mac went to court, and the city decided not to send in the bulldozers.

That Irish dynamo helped us save our neighbourhood, and she taught me a lesson too, about working together for what is right even when many people didn't agree with us. Sister Mac died last month. But the tree she planted is doing just great! It's going to grow in this neighbourhood for a long, long time, and we're not going to forget who put it there!

Hope for the Trees

Father Lou Quinn, of the Scarborough Foreign Mission Society, is a missionary in the Dominican Republic. He works with the people there to improve their lives. He is helping them replant the forests to end the soil erosion and other environmental damage that has occurred. Father Quinn also helps the people build houses and roads, and does whatever else he can to make their lives better.

Some years ago, as I was saying Mass, something unforgettable happened. Cachan, a developmentally handicapped member of our community, was passing in front of the altar just as I said, "The Lord be with you." He stopped in his tracks, turned to the altar, pointed at me and said in a strong voice, "That's the way it's gotta be!"

The people gathered at the Mass had all heard the blessing, "The Lord be with you," thousands of times, but never had it been so clear: the Lord has got to be with us, or we cannot live. Our faith teaches that God is in personal contact with creation all the time. We believe that God is truly present in

Father Lou Quinn working to improve people's lives.

the environment to strengthen, sustain and inspire us. Cachan recognized this perfectly.

Over the years, the memory of Cachan's response has strengthened our belief that the faith we profess must be based in our everyday lives. This is particularly important in San Jose de Ocoa, a parish in the mountains of the Dominican Republic. The land was once lush with forests and produced abundant food crops. Over many years the land was abused – mainly by the rich, but even by the poor. Forests were cut down. As a result, the good soil was eroded. Many of the poor farmers were forced from their farms in the lowlands, and began to farm the mountainsides. As they cut down more trees, even the poor mountain soils were washed away by the rains into the rivers, and the farmers were reduced to even greater poverty.

In the mid-1960s, I, together with other leaders in our community, began to preach on the unity between our faith and the replanting of forests and the conservation of the soil. Immediately we saw positive, if small, results. Later, other individuals and institutions began to support us in conservation projects. Most importantly, the people themselves became more aware of the urgent need to conserve our forests, rivers, soils, plants and animals. Before long, the entire community began to work on conservation projects, and to keep the environment in mind when developing various building projects like roads, schools and homes.

As a natural expression of the unity between our faith and the way we live in our natural world, we began to include different plants and trees among the offerings at the altar. After Mass, these plants were given to families throughout the area. Many thousands of trees have been planted in this way.

Sometimes our efforts to care for the environment were not as well received as we expected them to be. We were surprised by some of the opposition we met. We learned a valuable lesson: reforestation projects cannot succeed unless the people who live in the area are taken into account. Unless these people are convinced of God's call to work together to reforest and to conserve, old habits will return and the trees will disappear again. Every day we remind ourselves of the importance of including all members of the community and their vital needs in our conservation work.

Today, the people of San Jose de Ocoa face many challenges. Some are desperately poor. We have few medical and educational advantages. Our natural resources are often exploited for the benefit of a powerful, greedy few. Even so, we see ourselves as a community that is deeply blessed, because we are guided by our faith to live with each other and the environment in creative, life-sustaining ways. Most of all, we are blessed by Cachan's insight: The Lord is with us, and "that's the way its gotta be!"

What Can One Person Do?

In the middle of his Grade 7 year, David Grassby of Thornhill, Ontario, was working on a science fair project. After wondering about what was happening to the beautiful pond in his neighbourhood, and talking about it with friends, he set out to prove that one person with neither experience nor influence can bring about a change. The pond was gradually dying as a result of run-off containing pesticides and artificial fertilizers. There used to be lots of wildlife in the area. Now there was hardly any.

David gave several hundred questionnaires to the people in his town, wrote letters to key politicians and decision makers, got a little attention from the media and worked very hard. He proved that one person can make a difference: the mayor and the town council made some changes to protect the fragile ecosystems of the pond and the surrounding area.

With his success and the confidence to ask hard questions, David started his second project. He wanted to prove that a lot of motor oil (the little bit of oil left inside the "empty" small, plastic motor-oil containers you can get at every gas station in Canada) is spilled into landfill sites each year. First, David measured the leftover oil in 100 "empty" containers taken from the garbage cans of gas stations. Then he found out how many motor oil containers were sold in Canada the year before. He calculated that millions of litres of oil are spilled or dumped into landfill sites each year, and that nobody even knew it.

Again, with a bit of help from the media, David presented his findings to the president of a major oil firm. He asked the president to consider his suggestions for solving the problem. David's work caught the attention of David Suzuki, a well-known Canadian ecologist. Since then, young David has appeared several times on the CBC series *The Nature of Things* and has also taken part in many radio interviews and programs. He now co-hosts a regular television program on ecology for young people.

David loved a place that was "home" to him. This inspired him to move beyond feeling helpless about what was happening there. Maybe the greatest lesson David has given to others is that it is very important to know well the place where one lives, and to find the courage to fight to preserve it. By knowing a place well, we can have a deeper relationship with Earth, our "home."

The World That God Made

This is the world that God made.

These are God's people who live in the world that God made.

These are the luxuries for some of the people among God's people who live in the world that God made.

These are the factories that make the luxuries for some of the people among God's people who live in the world that God made.

This is the smoke that spews from the factories that make the luxuries for some of the people among God's people who live in the world that God made.

This is the rain that condenses from smoke that spews from the factories that make the luxuries for some of the people among God's people who live in the world that God made.

This is the acid that's in the rain that condenses from smoke that spews from the factories that make the luxuries for some of the people among God's people who live in the world that God made.

These are the rivers that foam with the acid that's in the rain that condenses from smoke that spews from the factories that make the luxuries for some of people among God's people who live in the world that God made.

This is the ocean that's poisoned by rivers that foam with the acid that's in the rain that condenses from smoke that spews from the factories that make the luxuries for some of the people among God's people who live in the world that God made.

These are the fish now beginning to die that live in the ocean that's poisoned by rivers that foam with the acid that's in the rain that condenses from smoke that spews from the factories that make the luxuries for some of the people among God's people who live in the world that God made.

These are the boats that no longer sail that caught the fish now beginning to die that live in the ocean that's poisoned by rivers that foam with the acid that's in the rain that condenses from smoke that spews from the factories that make the luxuries for some of the people among God's people who live in the world that God made.

This is the parent who cannot find work who worked on the boats that no longer sail that caught the fish now beginning to die that live in the ocean that's poisoned by rivers that foam with the acid that's in the rain that condenses from smoke that spews from the factories that make the luxuries for some of the people among God's people who live in the world that God made.

This is the family who must leave their home who love the parent who cannot find work who worked on the boats that no longer sail that caught the fish now beginning to die that live in the ocean that's poisoned by rivers that foam with the acid that's in the rain that condenses from smoke that spews from the factories that make the luxuries for some of the people among God's people who live in the world that God made.

These are the children now on the streets who come from the family who must leave their home who love the parent who cannot find work who worked on the boats that no longer sail that caught the fish now beginning to die that live in the ocean that's poisoned by rivers that foam with the acid that's in the rain that condenses from smoke that spews from the factories that make the luxuries for some of the people among God's people who live in the world that God made.

This is the Christian who's willing to change – live a simpler life – who sees the children now on the streets who come from the family who must leave their home who love the parent who cannot find work who worked on the boats that no longer sail that caught the fish now beginning to die that live in the ocean that's poisoned by rivers that foam with the acid that's in the rain that condenses from smoke that spews from the factories that make the luxuries for some of the people among God's people who live in the world that God made.

These are the luxuries no longer made. The cycle is broken because of the Christian who's willing to change – live a simpler life – who sees the children now on the streets who come from the family who must leave their home who love the parent who cannot find work who worked on the boats that no longer sail that caught the fish now beginning to die that live in the ocean that's poisoned by rivers that foam with the acid that's in the rain that condenses from smoke that spews from the factories that make the luxuries for some of the people among God's people who live in the world that God made.

Who is the Christian who's willing to change to care for the world that God made?

Canticle of the Creatures

May you be praised, O Lord, in all your
creatures,
especially brother sun, by whom you give us
light for the day;
he is beautiful, radiating great splendour,
and offering us a symbol of you, the Most
High....

May you be praised, my Lord, for sister water,
who is very useful and humble, precious and
chaste....

May you be praised, my Lord, for sister earth,
our mother,
who bears and feeds us,
and produces the variety of fruits and dappled
flowers and grasses....

Praise and bless my Lord, give thanks and serve
him in all humility.

St. Francis of Assisi

4.3 Why do I need you ?

Winkin', Blinkin': A Fable

A little girl was out digging in her sandbox, singing to herself. She liked the song. It was an old one she'd heard her grandmother sing:

"Winkin', Blinkin', I been thinkin',
What a grand world this would be,
If all the boys would be transported
Far across the great blue sea."

Her brother, playing in another part of the yard, heard her and hollered:

"Winkin', Blinkin', I been thinkin'
What a grand world this would be,
If all the *girls* would be transported
Far across the great blue sea."

This brother and sister got along well enough. They fought sometimes; at other times, they played together. Both of them had been known to wish that the other was a little more like themselves. The girl was sure that her brother was given special treatment just because he was a boy. She was sure that if she had a sister, life would be a lot fairer and a lot easier. The boy was equally sure that his sister had extra privileges because she was a girl. He thought that he would be misunderstood a lot less if there were no girls around to give his parents the wrong idea about what kids were really like.

"Winkin', Blinkin', I been thinkin'...." The little girl shouted the refrain back at her brother, standing and stamping her foot on the word "boys." Suddenly there was a loud crack of thunder. Without warning, the clear blue sky turned black, and the wind began to blow. The little girl grabbed her shovel and pail and began to run toward the house, calling for her brother to do the same.

As suddenly as it had started, the wind stopped and the sky cleared. The little girl looked around. Something was different. Her brother was gone! In his place was a little girl. The boys who had been playing soccer in a nearby field were also gone, replaced by a group of girls. The woman next door who had been mowing the lawn was still there, but now it was her daughter, not her husband, who was pruning the tree.

"Winkin', Blinkin', I been thinkin',
What a grand world..."

It had happened! She'd wished it and it had happened! All of the boys had been transported!

Once again she started running toward the house. But as she ran, her memories of boys began to fade away. By the time she reached the front door, the idea of a brother seemed like nothing more than a strange dream. There in the kitchen were her mother and grandmother and her brown-haired sister, the same three people she'd lived with all her life.

"Oh, there you are," her mom said as the little girl paused in the doorway. "We're just leaving to take your sister to her basketball practice. You help Grandma get dinner ready and we'll eat when I get home."

"It's not fair! Why do I have to help with dinner? She shouldn't get out of it just because she's got brown hair and mine's red!"

"Now stop that," her mother said. "You know that hair colour has nothing to do with this. She's on the team and you're not."

"Yeah, well her team only accepts brunettes!"

"Well, you could play on the redheads' team if you want to play so much," her sister chimed in.

"You think that just because you're a brunette you can tell me what to do! It's not fair and I won't listen." The little girl turned away crying.

Her sister began to sing in a quiet, taunting voice:

"Winkin', Blinkin', I been thinkin',
What a grand world this would be,
If all the redheads were transported
Far across the great blue sea."

The little girl stuck her fingers in her ears and sang back:

"Winkin', Blinkin', I been thinkin',
What a grand world this would be,
If all the *brunettes* were transported,
Far across..."

There was a loud peal of thunder and once again the wind began to blow....

When it stopped, the little girl found herself surrounded by redheads. And there was her short, redheaded sister, sticking out her tongue when their mother wasn't looking, and whispering:

"Winkin', Blinkin', I been thinkin',
What a grand world this would be,
If all the tall kids were transported
Far across the great blue sea."

Of course, the little girl responded by wishing that all the short kids would be transported. Once again, she heard the thunder and saw the black sky.

And so it went. Over and over again, the little girl found herself in places where she felt that life would be better if everyone was a little more like her in one way or another. Over and over again, she wished away those who were different. And over and over, with a crash of thunder and a blast of wind, her wish was granted. Before long, the little girl had wished away everyone but herself. Not surprisingly, she was bored and lonely.

She began to have some very strange dreams. She dreamed of a world in which there were other people, all kinds of other people, people of many heights and many sizes, people with different interests and skills, people of different colours and even people of different genders! When she woke up, she began to tell herself about her dream. (After all, there was no one else to tell.) "Boys..." she said to herself. "I wonder where I got such a funny idea. What a grand world it would be if they really did exist."

And the wind began to blow....

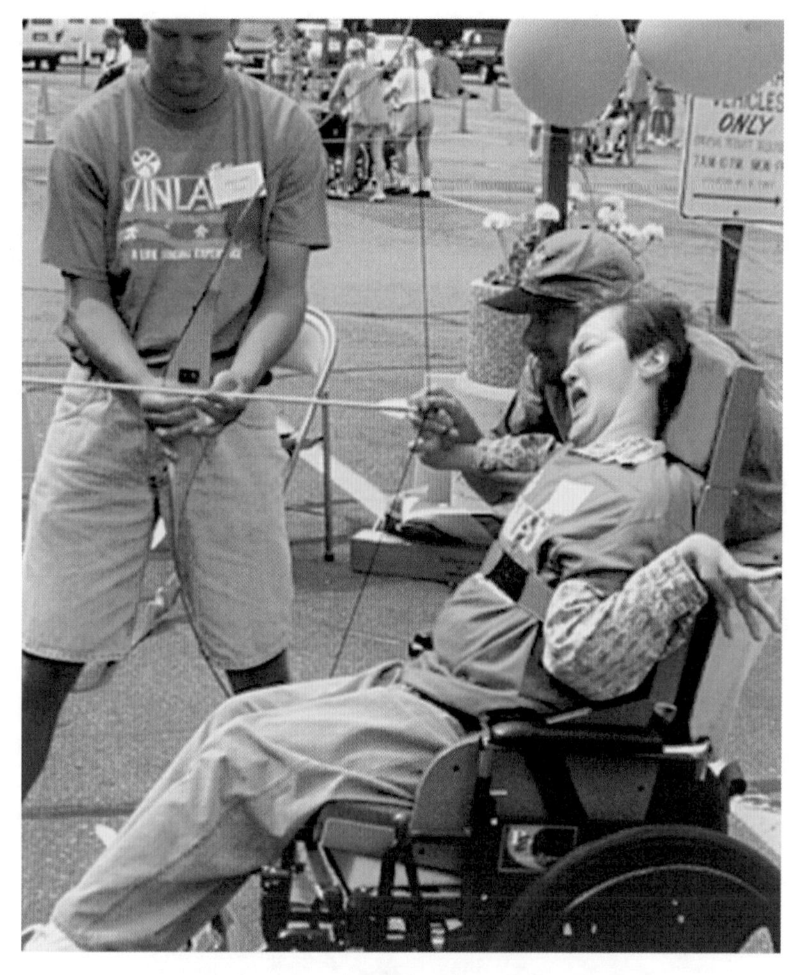

What Are They Worth?

We all know in our hearts what the little girl in the fable learned: the world would not be a better place if we got rid of all the people who are different from us. Some "types" of people are not worth more than other "types" of people. Human beings are created in the image and likeness of an infinite God who knows endless variety. Should we be surprised that there are endless varieties among us?

We have value as human beings – not because we have certain qualities that other humans have or value, but because we have qualities that no other humans have and that God values.

This may be easier to understand if we think about two Grade 8 students, Kim and Jason. Both of them are often misunderstood and valued for the wrong reasons. Many think that Kim has value as a person because of her "perfect" body and "gorgeous" hair and because she has already earned money as a model. In truth, Kim is valuable because she loves and is loved by her grandmother, with whom she lives. Her value is in her laughter, which makes others smile. It's in her loud singing when she's home all alone. Kim's value is too great to be measured because God has no other daughters exactly like her.

Those who think Kim's value is based on her being a model often think that Jason's value is based on his being in a wheelchair and on his inability to spell his own name on bad days. But Jason's value is in his ability to make his brother smile when no one else can. It's in the fact that his birth made his parents slow down and start enjoying life more. It's in his appreciation for the wonder of a spider spinning a web. Jason's value is too great to be measured because God has no other sons exactly like him.

Our uniqueness lets each of us take part in God's creation in a way that no one else can. The uniqueness of each person makes it possible for him or her to work with God in shaping creation. When we value other people because they are unique, we are treating them with the dignity they deserve. When we leave people out or make fun of them because they are different from us, we are hurting their dignity and insulting God.

Male and Female in God's Image

Whenever two human beings work together, they produce something new – something that could not have come from either one alone. Whenever this happens, creation takes place and God's plan for creation is brought closer to completion.

If human beings are to be as creative as we can be, we need one another. We need all the creativity that comes when we join with people who see and do things in ways that are different from ours. The clearest example of this is the joining together of a husband and wife. Two people who are different from each other produce a child who is a new and unique person. In making us male and female, and in making the union of male and female needed for the creation of children, God made it clear that differences are not only good, they are necessary. These differences should help us respect and care for one another more, not less.

In the beginning, God did not choose to create two beings who were exactly alike. God did not decide that the perfect partner for Adam would be an exact copy of Adam. Instead, God chose someone who was both like and unlike Adam. God's gift of maleness and femaleness reminds us that God does not want us all to be the same. We should never try to be just like someone else. We should never try to make someone else be just like us. We should never leave people out just because they are different from us.

Litany of the Saints

The litany is a very old form of prayer. This prayer is led by one member of the community. The rest of the community responds with a refrain.

Shorter forms of the litany are part of the Mass. Two of these are "Lord, have mercy. Christ, have mercy. Lord, have mercy" and "Lamb of God, who takes away the sins of the world, have mercy on us."

The litany of the saints started in the early church. Christian communities would name people who had been killed because of their faith, or who had been very holy men and women, and ask these people to pray for them. The Christian community believes that those who have died are still part of the community. That means they can pray for us and we can pray for them.

The litany is often sung. It is part of the liturgy for the Easter Vigil, baptisms and ordinations. As we pray the litany of the saints, we are reminded that we are part of a community that includes people who have lived before us. It reminds us that we need and look out for one another.

Litany of the Saints

Cantor	All
Lord, have mercy. Christ, have mercy. Lord, have mercy.	Lord, have mercy. Christ, have mercy. Lord, have mercy.
Holy Mary, Mother of God,	pray for us. *(repeat for each of the following lines)*
Saint Michael, Holy angels of God, Abraham and Sarah, Moses, Ruth and Elijah, Saint Joachim and Saint Anne, Saint Joseph, Saint Elizabeth, Saint John the Baptist, Saint Peter and Saint Paul, Saint Mary Magdalene, Saint Stephen,	

Saint Lawrence,
Saint Jean de Brébeuf, Saint Isaac Jogues
and the holy Canadian Martyrs,
Saint Perpetua and Saint Felicity,
Saint Agnes,
Saint Gregory,
Saint Augustine,
Saint Monica,
Saint Basil,
Saint Olga and Saint Vladimir,
Saint Catherine of Sienna,
Saint Teresa of Jesus,
Saint Martin de Porres,
Saint Rose of Lima,
Blessed François de Laval,
Saint Benedict,
Saint Francis, Saint Claire and Saint Dominic,
Saint John Vianney,
Saint Marguerite Bourgeoys,
Saint Marguerite d'Youville,
Saint Kizito,
Saint Elizabeth Seton,
Saint Paul Chong Hasang
Blessed Kateri Tekakwitha,
All holy men and women.

Lord, be merciful. — Lord, save your people.
From all harm,
From every sin,
From all temptations,
From everlasting death,

By your coming among us, — Lord, save your people.
By your death and rising to new life,
By your gift of the Holy Spirit,

Be merciful to us sinners, — Lord, hear our prayer.

Jesus, Son of the living God. — Lord, hear our prayer.

Christ, hear us. — Christ, hear us.

Lord Jesus, hear our prayer. — Lord Jesus, hear our prayer.

Unit 4 Summary Statements

- God creates for people and with people.
- People are called to co-operate with God by loving and helping complete the work of creation.
- We co-operate with God by caring for each other and caring for the world around us.
- Each of us has gifts that are needed in order for creation to unfold according to God's plan.
- God creates from nothing.
- All creation is good.
- We are stewards (caretakers) of creation.
- Faith and science do not need to be in conflict. Both are searching for truth, and all truth comes from God. The issues that concern scientists the most may be different from the issues that concern those seeking faith the most; therefore, they focus on different things.
- The environmental crisis is a result of our being unwilling to live justly.
- Human beings were created to share, give and love. Our lives are not complete if we are always isolated from each other.
- In all that he did, Jesus showed that people who were "different" deserved to be loved and included.
- We are called to challenge anything that hurts our dignity or the dignity of others.
- God created us male and female in the divine image. Humanity is not complete unless it is both male and female.

Key Terms

creation
Creator
stewardship
Genesis
human dignity
procreation
litany
co-operating in creation

Unit 5

We believe in Jesus Christ, his only Son

5.1 What's in a name?

What's in a Name?

I think his name was Carl, but I'm really not sure. When I got to camp, the guys in my tent told me that his nickname was Loser. Whenever he came near, someone was sure to start up that little sing-song chant: "Dah... Which way did 'e go? Which way did 'e go? Dah...." I knew right away that this was not a guy I wanted to get stuck with on a camping trip.

But, just my luck, he was on my wilderness trip, and he did his best to live up to his nickname. He must have lost half of our group's camping gear – things like pots and pans, a tent pole, our can opener.... He'd go to wash something, or use it or put it away, then he'd think about something else, set the thing down under a tree, behind a rock, or wherever, and forget about it! I thought our counsellor was going to go crazy the day he carried our stove down by the water and left it where the incoming tide could (and did) cover it. He said that he "just wanted to pick some wild blueberries for the group."

Whatever the group was talking about, Loser would join in with some comment that didn't have anything to do with it. At least, I'm pretty sure it didn't. I don't really remember much of what he said. Whenever he opened his mouth, someone would whisper, "Dah.... Which way did 'e go?" and we'd all be too busy trying not to laugh to pay much attention to him.

When I went back to the same camp the next summer, I wasn't too sad to learn that Loser wasn't there. I figured I could probably have hot food for a whole trip. There'd be no one to lose the food, the stove or the pots!

At the end of that second summer, we went to visit family friends whose daughter had spent the summer at a different camp. We were sharing stories and looking at photos when she pulled out a picture of Loser. Before I could say anything, she said, "You should meet this guy."

Then she said, "When I first got to camp, I heard about somebody called Doc.

Everyone wanted him on their trips. I knew just from his name that he was probably the kind of guy who makes a trip a lot easier. You know, the kind who can start fires with wet wood or whatever. I was glad when they put him in my group. He was great! Even better than I expected. We got lost at one point on our trip and everyone was tired and hungry. Doc started showing us all the different wild things we could eat to survive. At night this guy could keep us all entertained, or terrified, with the world's best ghost stories! I swear, he could make anyone believe anything. On top of it all, he's got a great sense of humour. I never met anyone who was so willing to laugh at himself. There were times when he'd have so many ideas buzzing around in his head that he'd forget the most basic things, but then he'd turn it into one big joke on himself. We almost looked forward to the times when he misplaced something because he could turn finding it again into a great game."

She paused for a minute, and I knew it was coming: "I just remembered – he said that he was at your camp last summer. Do you know him?"

Reflection questions

1. How did Carl's nicknames influence those who met him?
2. How do names shape what we expect of people?
3. How do names and titles influence how we observe people?

Titles

We give people titles to show respect for what they do in our society. Experts in medicine are called "Doctor," a judge is "Your Honour," a priest is "Father," and the Pope is "Your Holiness." Often titles do more than show respect: they say what a person is or does. Titles may also say something about our relationship with different people. For example, even if your mother is a judge, you will probably call her "Mom" more often than you will call her "Your Honour." The title "Mom" indicates that you expect far more from this judge than you would from any other.

Your Highness

Chief

Your Holiness

The titles given to Jesus tell us who he is and what he has come to do. We call Jesus by different titles at different times, depending on our relationship with him.

For most of his life, Jesus seemed to be an ordinary smalltown craftsman. None of his neighbours knew he was special. (Remember that the events at his birth and when he was 12 years old happened far away from Nazareth and were not written up until much later.)

So the townspeople were very surprised when, at age 30, Jesus stepped out of his workshop and began to proclaim the coming of the kingdom of God. Some people thought he was crazy or evil.

Others, however, were attracted by the beauty and power of his teaching, and by the wonders of healing that he did. They tried to find titles to describe Jesus and the new relationships they had with him. Each of the titles they used means something special.

The Titles of Jesus

Rabbi

Jesus was never a professional rabbi who taught in a synagogue. But he taught with authority (more strongly than the rabbis, Matthew 7.29 says), and he had a group of disciples who followed him. So people often did address him as "Rabbi," which means teacher.

When we call Jesus "Rabbi" or teacher, we are reminded that he helps us to understand what God wants of us. We believe that Jesus can and does show us how to live life to the full.

Jesus was a great teacher, but he had more authority than any other teacher, and he did far more than just teach us about God. For that reason, "Rabbi" doesn't say everything about Jesus.

Priest

Jesus was not a Catholic priest. He was not a Jewish priest, either – that is, he did not earn his living working in the Temple. But we still call him the "Great High Priest." The role of the priest was to offer a sacrifice to God on behalf of all the people. The sacrifice showed the people's desire to give their best to God and to turn away from anything that kept them apart from God. Jesus died because he could not stay faithful to God if he avoided death. Jesus truly gave his

very best to God, and he did it for us. Jesus' life and death were for us. He lived and died to reunite human beings with God, so that no matter how bad things get, one person (Jesus) stays faithful to God on behalf of all people.

When we call Jesus a priest, we celebrate the fact that he offered the sacrifice of his life – not for his own sake, but for the sake of all people.

Jesus is a high priest who offers the perfect sacrifice: the sacrifice that pleases God. He also restores the good relationship between God and humanity. But Jesus is much more than a priest.

Lamb of God

Jesus not only offered a sacrifice on behalf of all people, Jesus was (and is) the sacrifice. The Temple sacrifice was usually a lamb. When a lamb was offered in the Temple, the people believed that peace was restored between God and God's people who had sinned. We call Jesus the "Lamb of God" because he is the sacrifice that restores peace between God and us when we have sinned.

When we call Jesus the Lamb of God, we remember that he gave everything for us even though we did not deserve it. We celebrate the fact that God protects and cares for us and has done so ever since the Exodus from Egypt. We remember that even the gifts we give to God and to one another were given to us first by God.

Prophet

The prophets were great preachers and poets who spoke the word of God to God's people.

Usually their preaching attacked kings, priests and other people for not being faithful to the law of God. The prophets kept reminding the Jewish people that justice and mercy were more important to God than religious celebrations and expensive offerings in the Temple. Because the prophets criticized them, many people hated them. But the people still realized that what the prophets were saying was true, and kept the prophets' teachings as part of the Sacred Scriptures.

Some parts of Jesus' teachings were like the prophets' teachings. Many people thought he was a prophet, and gave him that title of honour. Jesus was a prophet, and we know that he spoke the words of God. But Jesus was much more than a prophet, too.

Messiah – Christ

The Jewish people believed that God would send them a great leader. They called him "The Anointed One" (in Hebrew, *Messiah*; in Greek, *Christos*) because they used to anoint their leaders with oil as a sign of God's favour and of the ruler's authority. (Today we anoint with oil at baptism, at confirmation, during the anointing of the sick and at the ordination of a priest.)

The Messiah was expected to be a descendant of King David. He would be a political leader who would make Israel a free kingdom, but mostly he would be a spiritual leader, sent by God to help the people be true and faithful believers. The Jewish people didn't expect the Messiah to be God's own divine Son.

When Jesus proclaimed the coming of God's kingdom with such power, many people hoped he was the Messiah.

Jesus didn't like to be called Messiah (or Christ), probably because people who called

him that would expect him to act like an earthly king (see Mark 8.29-30 and John 6.15). He later accepted the title of Messiah (see Mark 14.62). After his resurrection, it became such a popular title for him that now we use the word "Christ" almost as if it were his last name.

With the death and resurrection of Jesus, the title "Christ" lost its political meaning. We now know that our "king" is not one who shows off his authority and forces people to obey, but one who serves others and, by his own example, teaches them how to love.

The Messiah was expected to be anointed by God as priest, prophet and king. Jesus did come as priest, prophet and king. He was the fulfillment of the Jewish hopes, even though he was not what most Jews expected. He was indeed the Messiah – but he was more than the Messiah, too.

Son of David

People sometimes ask, "If Jesus was from the family of David, wouldn't he be a prince?" The answer is no. David lived a thousand years before Jesus, and he had dozens of children (by many different wives). One of his sons became king after he died, and the rest of David's children stayed politically unimportant. After a few generations, his many descendants would always remember that they could trace their family roots back to David, but they were ordinary poor people.

The Jewish people believed that the Messiah would come from the house (or family) of David because long before, God had promised that David's house and his kingdom would last forever (2 Samuel 7.16). When Jesus is called the Son of David, that ancient promise is remembered. When believers call Jesus "Son of David," they are showing that they believe in God's faithfulness. God promised a son of David who would end their misery; Jesus is the fulfillment of that promise.

Jesus the Nazarene

What was Jesus' last name if it wasn't "Christ"? Family names in Jesus' day were not set the way ours are now. Jesus' last name probably changed during his lifetime.

As he grew up, he would be called "Jesus, son of Joseph," because most children were named this way.

After Joseph died, Jesus might have been named by the work he did ("Carpenter"?).

And after he left his hometown, Jesus would be named for the place he came from. This was the name the soldiers put up when he was on the cross: Jesus of Nazareth.

Jesus' first name also has a special meaning. In Hebrew, it is "Joshua." It's an ordinary name, but it means "God saves." So even Jesus' name tells about what he has done for us.

On the cross, *I N R I*, a Latin inscription, stands for:

Iesus	Jesus
Nazarenus	of Nazareth
Rex	King
Iudaerorum	of the Jews

Saviour

We often refer to Jesus as our saviour because we believe that his death and resurrection have saved us from the power of death. Because of the resurrection of Jesus, death has no permanent power. God's love is stronger than death, so death cannot keep people apart from love or from God. Without Jesus, people could not go beyond death into eternal life with God. Without Jesus, death would have kept human beings apart from God forever. Sin, which keeps us apart from God, would have won out. But because of Jesus, death is only a transition point from one way of knowing God to another. So we say that Jesus saves us from being kept apart from God because Jesus saves us from sin and death.

Son of Man

According to the gospels, Jesus often referred to himself as the "Son of Man." It is a surprising and unusual title, and it has two almost opposite meanings at the same time.

Jesus called himself Son of Man when he spoke about the sufferings and death that he expected to go through. This title stresses that he was a human person like us who realized that he was going to die. He understood his death as being so important that it was like part of his name.

Jesus also called himself Son of Man when he spoke of the future, when he would return in glory, "riding on the clouds of heaven" with great power and majesty. That image is from the Book of Daniel (7.14), which tells about the glorious end of the Age. The Son of Man is connected with the final judgement of all people. When this title is used in the New Testament, we are reminded that it is Jesus who will judge us.

Lord

In Jesus' time, the word "lord" didn't mean much more than the polite word "sir" or "master" (which the Israelites called their rabbis).

But when the Jewish people read the Scriptures, they always called God "The Lord" (with a capital L). In Greek, the word for Lord is *Kyrios*. After Jesus rose from the dead, his disciples began to call him Lord with a capital L (see Acts 2.36 and Philippians 2.11). By that title, they meant that he was not only a human being, but also God. That is what Thomas meant when he called Jesus, "My Lord and my God!" (John 20.28).

Son of God

People were often called "son of God" in the Hebrew Scriptures. It meant that they were favoured by God, that God blessed them and helped them. All the people of Israel were called sons of God; the kings were called sons of God in a special way. But Jesus did things that amazed people, and made them think that he was Son of God in a way that was different from everyone else. He taught with such confidence and beauty. He even dared to say that the law God had given on Mount Sinai must be made deeper and stronger if God's will were truly to be done. Jesus forgave people's sins, which only God can do. He healed people and even brought dead people back to life. He dared to name God as his "Father" in a way that no other Jew had ever done. He invited other people to do this, too.

After Jesus rose from the dead, his followers grew to understand even more clearly that Jesus was not just a great human being. He is divine; he shares the being of God. Somehow, in Jesus, God walked around on earth in person and lived a single human life. The title "Son of God" came to mean that Jesus, even though he lived and died as a human being, is not one of God's creatures. He has been one with God since the very beginning of time. When we call Jesus "Son of God," we show that we believe that when we relate to Jesus, we are relating to God.

That is why Son of God is the greatest title we have for Jesus, and often the first one that we use.

The Jesus Prayer

"Lord, Jesus Christ, Son of God, have mercy on me, a sinner."

5.2 How does Jesus challenge me?

The Eagle in the Chicken Coop

There's an old story about a farmer who found an eagle's egg and brought it home. He put it in one of the nests in his chicken coop. The hen sat on it along with her other eggs and kept it warm until it hatched.

The young eagle born in the chicken coop assumed that she was a chicken. She learned to scratch the ground and peck for grubs and seeds. She learned to flap her wings a little bit as she hopped from the ground to the fence, or the fence to the ground; and she learned to waddle around, shaking her tail feathers and squawking whenever the rooster came into the yard. She did all of the things that a chicken was expected to do.

One day, the young eagle looked up and saw a majestic bird soaring high overhead. "Who is that?" she asked, her voice filled with awe.

"That is Eagle, the most powerful of all the birds," one of the older chickens explained. "He can go anywhere he wishes to go. No one can ever fence him in."

The young eagle sighed. "I wish I could be like that. Do you suppose I could...."

"Forget it." Another chicken joined the conversation. "You're just a chicken like the rest of us. No one expects us to do any more than squawk and lay eggs, and for good reason – that's all we're really capable of. Chickens are supposed to flap their wings and hop. If one of us started actually trying to fly, let alone trying to soar like an eagle, the farmer would be sure to think that some terrible disease had infested his chickens. We'd all be on our way to the slaughterhouse! Every chicken has a responsibility to behave as she's expected to behave. That's what makes the coop a safe place to live."

"I suppose you're right," the young eagle said, nodding. Then she scratched the ground and pecked at another grub.

And so the eagle lived and died as a chicken because that's what everyone, including the eagle herself, expected her to do.

Background for Understanding the Bible

The Sabbath

In Jesus' time, people understood the third commandment, "Keep holy the Sabbath," to mean that they should not work on the Sabbath. Different communities interpreted this rule in different ways. Everyone agreed that certain things were always forbidden: people were not allowed to do those things that they did to earn a living; they were not allowed to chop wood, kindle a fire or cook;[1] and they were not allowed to take a life, even the life of a bug. There were other issues that caused a lot more argument, especially between the two groups that were most concerned about preserving all of the Jewish laws: the pharisees and the Essenes.

The pharisees believed that people were allowed to do things they needed to do to preserve life. For example, a person was allowed to rescue an animal from a ditch even on the Sabbath. The Essenes believed that no one was allowed to do anything that took physical effort on the Sabbath, even if there was a good reason for doing it. For example, a person could never lift an animal on the Sabbath, even if that animal had fallen into a well and would drown if it was not lifted out. Both groups believed that no one was allowed to do anything that could wait until the next day.

[1] Those who did not earn money but who worked at home doing things needed for day-to-day survival were also entitled to a day of rest.

The Sabbath traditions were one of the main things that made the Jews different from the people around them. The pharisees and the Essenes wanted to be sure that the Sabbath laws were interpreted correctly. Both groups believed that if Jews, like the Gentiles around them, worked on the Sabbath, their faith and their relationship with God would not survive.

Leprosy

Hansen's disease, or leprosy (as it is called in the Bible), is a contagious disease that was feared very much in Jesus' time. Bacteria attack the nerves of a person who has leprosy. This causes a loss of feeling and even blindness. A secondary, and the most visible, effect of the disease is that the person's arms and legs can become deformed. Arms and legs may be so damaged that they have to be cut off. Leprosy also causes scaly patches on the skin. Although it can now

be cured with drugs, leprosy is still a medical problem in some parts of the world.

When the man in Matthew's gospel was told that he had leprosy, he could not work at his job anymore, and he had to go and live outside the town in a camp full of other people who had the disease. He had to leave his home and family right away, without even kissing them goodbye. Leprosy was such a hopeless illness that a leper's family thought of him or her as already dead.

When a leper came near another person, the leper had to yell, "Unclean, unclean," to warn the other person to stay away. A Jew who touched a leper would be seen as ritually unclean. He or she would have to go through a purification process before being allowed to take part in community activities. That usually meant being alone for a time to keep the disease from spreading.

Tax Collectors

In first-century Palestine, where Jesus lived, taxes were collected from all of the Jews and sent to Rome to support the government of the emperor. People bid for the job of tax collector. Each bidder would tell the Roman authorities how much he thought he could collect from the Jews. The person who promised the most money would get the job.

Tax collectors could charge the people as much as they thought they could get. They gave whatever they had promised to the Romans and kept the rest.

Most people in the Jewish community hated the tax collectors. They saw tax collectors as traitors and sinners because they co-operated with the Roman occupiers in the hopes of getting rich. They were willing to rob their own people to support a foreign government (that treated the Jews badly) and a pagan god.

Pious Jews did not have anything to do

Doogie Dogma

(Catechism #515, 516 & #518)

with tax collectors. They believed that spending time with people who had no regard for God and for God's law would weaken their own relationship with God. The pharisees and their followers would not share a meal with a tax collector because to do so would show that they accepted both the person and his behaviour.

They couldn't even justify spending time with a tax collector in the hope that he might change. The pharisees believed that it was not possible for tax collectors to truly convert. Sinners who wished to repent of their sins and take part in community activities again had to make up for the damage they had done. Tax collectors were believed to have cheated so many people that it was impossible for them to make up for what they had done. For this reason, they could not repent and be welcomed back into the community.

Women

In Jesus' day, it was very unusual for a woman to study religious matters. Men could become disciples of holy teachers. They sat at the feet of their instructors to learn about the ways of God. Women were rarely allowed to study in this way. Many rabbis taught that women should not be allowed to learn any more than the most basic things about faith. During religious services, women had to sit in a separate section from the men; they could not take part fully in religious services. Women were usually expected to do the housework.

When Jesus visits Mary and Martha (Luke 10.38-42), Mary sits at Jesus' feet as a disciple and Jesus teaches her about God. Martha complains because Mary is not doing what women are "supposed" to do – helping with the household chores.

Jesus' friendship with Mary and Martha and with many other women was very unusual. It is significant that Jesus thought that women as well as men deserved to hear the Good News. He was not following his society's ideas about teaching women.

It is worth noting that the first person Jesus appeared to after his resurrection was a woman. Jesus spoke with Mary Magdalene and then sent her to tell the apostles that he was alive. Mary Magdalene is often called "the apostle to the apostles." Jesus not only taught women, he expected them to teach others.

Father, you so loved the world
that in the fullness of time
you sent your only Son to be our Saviour.
He was conceived
through the power of the Holy Spirit,
and born of the Virgin Mary,
a man like us in all things but sin.

To the poor he proclaimed the good news of
salvation,
to prisoners, freedom,
and to those in sorrow, joy.
In fulfillment of your will
he gave himself up to death;
but by rising from the dead,
he destroyed death and restored life.

And that we might live
no longer for ourselves but for him,
he sent the Holy Spirit from you, Father,
as his first gift to those who believe,
to complete his work on earth
and bring us the fullness of grace.

from Eucharistic Prayer IV

5.3 What makes Jesus believable?

I Believe

A teenage girl was asked by some of her classmates, "Do you seriously believe in Jesus or do you just do this church stuff because your parents make you do it?"

She responded immediately, "Oh, I really believe in Jesus. I think of him as my friend."

"Your friend! Do you even really know him? How old is he?"

"I can't really answer that."

"What are his favourite hobbies?

"I don't know."

"Where is his house? Where did he go to school? What is his favourite colour?"

"I don't know the answer to any of those questions. They're just not that important!"

"If you don't know anything about Jesus, how can you call him a friend?"

"I didn't say that I don't know anything about him. I do know the things that are really important. I know that a few years ago my parents were fighting all the time. My dad was laid off and my mom got really sick. I know that I was failing school, my friends all seemed to abandon me and I was thinking about ending everything. Then friends invited us to church.

"We started to pray more. My folks stopped fighting. People in the church helped Dad find several temporary jobs until he finally found a permanent one. I realized that one of the reasons my friends had stopped spending time with me was that I spent so much time complaining and criticizing other people and so little time listening or doing kind things. I made a real effort to change. I started listening more and complaining less. I made a lot of new friends. My mom is still sick but I know that praying with our family and with some friends from church has made life a lot easier for her. Because we believe that God will be with us no matter what happens, my family no longer needs to pretend that Mom isn't really sick. Since we started praying together, we talk a lot more and fight a lot less.

"I may not know Jesus' favourite colour, but I do know that he's made me a better person and my family a better family. That's why I believe in him and call him friend."

To believe in Jesus is to let him change our lives.

IHЦI
IC
XC

Lord, to whom can we go?

[Jesus'] disciples…said, "This teaching is difficult; who can accept it?"

Jesus said…"It is the spirit that gives life…. The words that I have spoken to you are spirit and life. But among you there are some who do not believe." For Jesus knew from the first who were the ones that did not believe, and who was the one that would betray him. And he said, "For this reason I have told you that no one can come to me unless it is granted by the Father."

Because of this many of his disciples turned back and no longer went about with him. So Jesus asked the twelve, "Do you also wish to go away?"

Simon Peter answered him, "Lord, to whom can we go? You have the words of eternal life. We have come to believe and know that you are the Holy One of God."

John 6.60-69

Unit 5 Summary Statements

- The name Jesus means "God saves." Jesus' name tells us both his identity and his mission.
- When we name someone or give someone a title, we make a relationship with that person.
- We call Jesus "the Lamb of God" because he is the sacrifice that restores peace between God and us when we sin.
- Messiah means "anointed one." People expected the Messiah to be anointed by God as priest, prophet and king. Jesus was all of those, though not in the way most people had expected the Messiah to be. Jesus was the Messiah but he was also more than the Messiah.
- "Son of God" is probably the best title we have for Jesus. Jesus is not one of God's creatures, but has been one with God since the beginning of time. Jesus can help us understand God's love in a way that no other person ever could.
- Jesus challenged some of the structures of power in society. He always said that people were more important than rules.
- Jesus encouraged people to rethink some of their beliefs about God and about other people.
- Jesus invites all people, but especially sinners and outcasts, to share in God's love and to experience God's blessings.
- Religious images can help us to express and deepen our relationship with Jesus.
- In biblical times, people had life-changing meetings with Jesus, both before and after his death and resurrection. Such life-changing meetings with Jesus have kept happening in the centuries since his resurrection.
- Through his actions, Jesus reveals God's care for us.

Key Terms

rabbi	Son of David	Sabbath
priest	saviour	Lord
Lamb of God	Son of Man	Messiah
prophet	Son of God	

Unit 6
We believe in Jesus...our Lord

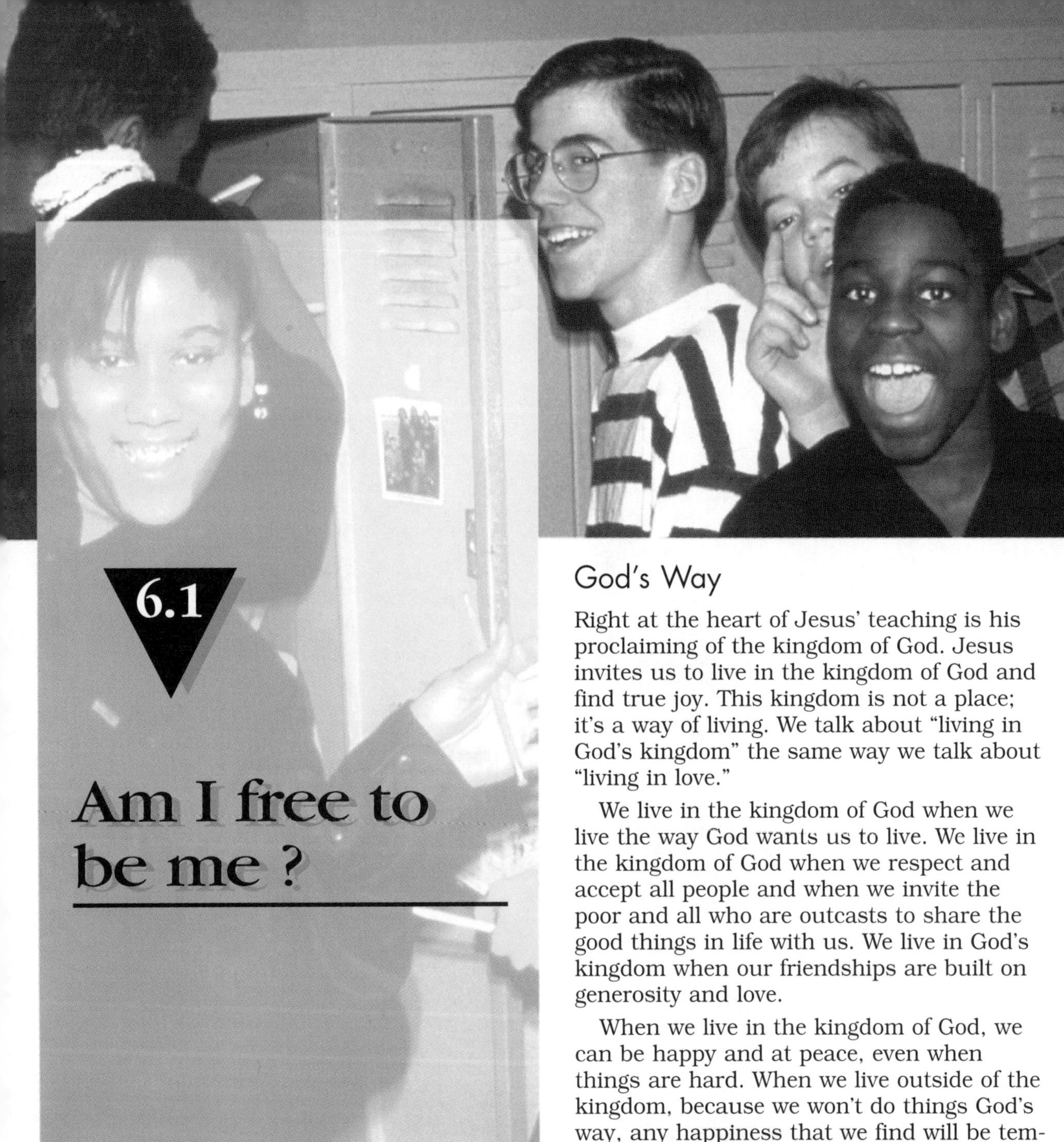

6.1

Am I free to be me ?

God's Way

Right at the heart of Jesus' teaching is his proclaiming of the kingdom of God. Jesus invites us to live in the kingdom of God and find true joy. This kingdom is not a place; it's a way of living. We talk about "living in God's kingdom" the same way we talk about "living in love."

We live in the kingdom of God when we live the way God wants us to live. We live in the kingdom of God when we respect and accept all people and when we invite the poor and all who are outcasts to share the good things in life with us. We live in God's kingdom when our friendships are built on generosity and love.

When we live in the kingdom of God, we can be happy and at peace, even when things are hard. When we live outside of the kingdom, because we won't do things God's way, any happiness that we find will be temporary. As soon as things go wrong, that kind of happiness will disappear.

None of us lives completely in the kingdom of God right now, but most of us do have moments when we live in the kingdom, moments when we do things God's way and find deep happiness and peace. We call Jesus "Lord" because we believe that he can give us this happiness and peace – not just once in a while, but in everything we do. We believe that Jesus is "in charge" of the kingdom of God. Without Jesus' invitation, we would have no right to share in the joy of the kingdom. Without Jesus' guidance, we would not know *how* to share in that joy.

Jesus teaches us, through both his words and his example, how to live according to God's way and how to enter the kingdom of God. He helps us build the kinds of relationships God wants us to build, the kind where we are really free to be ourselves. If we agree to live in the kingdom where Jesus is Lord, we will be free to be the people we were created to be.

When we use the title "Lord," we are saying that we want to live in that kingdom. We are saying that we are willing to accept God's way. We are also saying that no one has the authority to expect us to act in a way that goes against God's way. "Lord" is a title given to a ruler who has total power to decide what is right and wrong for his subjects. When we call Jesus "Lord," we accept Jesus' teachings about the right and the wrong way to live.

God's Way Versus the Devil's Way

Before Jesus called any of the disciples, he spent 40 days in the desert fasting and praying. At the end of that time, the devil came and tempted him. The devil tried to convince him that God's way was not the best way. The devil tried to get Jesus to stop building his relationships on love and trust, which takes a lot of time. The devil said that Jesus could get all of the attention and respect he could want by giving up God's way and tricking people.

Jesus turned down the devil's temptations. He knew that true success and happiness would only be possible if he lived

according to God's way. Jesus made it clear that any relationship worth having must be rooted in genuine sharing and co-operation, not abuse and power. Jesus showed us that God's way is not the way of quick and easy answers, but of genuine and patient love.

Prayer, Fasting and Abstinence

After he was baptized by John the Baptist, Jesus spent 40 days in the desert fasting and praying. Fasting means eating less food to strengthen one's spiritual life. By controlling our physical appetites, we weaken their power over us. In early times, fasting meant not eating any food for part of the fast day or for the whole day. Today, it usually means eating one modest main meal and two smaller ones in a day. "Abstinence" means not eating meat or some other luxury food for a period of time.

"The fifth precept [of the Church], 'You shall observe the prescribed days of fasting and abstinence,'...helps us acquire mastery over our instincts and freedom of heart" (*Catechism of the Catholic Church*, #2043).

The tradition of the Church calls for abstinence from meat, or from some other food, on Fridays. The Church calls for both abstinence and fasting on Ash Wednesday and Good Friday. The law of abstinence is for people who are over age 14. The law of fasting is for adults.

If you can observe the laws of fasting and abstinence from time to time without hurting your health, try to get into the habit. As a class, you might try abstaining from all junk food and fasting from snacks for a day. Offer this up to God as a prayer, asking for forgiveness and for spiritual strength. In your prayer, ask God, "Am I free to be me?" Prayer and occasional self-denial, such as fasting, will help you become more free to become the best that you can be.

6.2

What do I need to be happy?

Who Could Be Happy Here?

Nadine arrived at camp looking for a fight. I overheard her talking to her parents while she waited in line for her health check. I didn't hear what her mother said, but no one could miss Nadine's response: "What's there to be happy about? This place is a dump and everyone here looks like they buy their clothes at Kmart. You wouldn't catch me dead in clothes like that."

A little while later, I watched as Nadine went to her tent. She took one look inside and threw her bags on the ground. "I don't believe this! I come here to have a good time. I think camp is a place where I could be happy, and look what happens. I get stuck with a top bunk in a scummy old tent where every time I sit up I'm going to get a face full of either spider webs or mildew. This is just great!"

Her counsellor tried to be friendly. She pointed out that it wasn't really mildew on the tent; the black spots were just stains where mildew had been scrubbed off. The counsellor then offered to help rearrange the beds a bit so that the top bunks wouldn't be as close to the roof of the tent. "Oh, get out of my face!" Nadine snapped. "You sound just like my mother, always willing to make do. This place is going to be just tons of fun; I can tell already."

Nadine picked up one of her bags and dumped it into the centre of the tent. She yanked open the zipper and pulled out a can of pop and a huge bag of chips. Just at that moment, one of the other girls in her tent walked up. "Hi. I haven't met you yet. My name is Kerry."

"No, you can't have any of my food, so don't bother asking. And watch where you're stepping! You just kicked my bag. For your information, that's expensive European luggage, not some cheap garbage like everyone else has."

"What... What are you talking about? I didn't kick your bag and I don't want your food. I was trying to be friendly."

"Well, bug off, why don't you. I don't need friends who are looking for handouts. Just because I have more snack food than the rest of you losers put together, you think you have a right to ask for some."

Kerry didn't say a word. She just turned and walked away from the tent. Two of the other girls from the tent were coming down the path. They stopped for a minute when they saw Kerry. Kerry whispered something and pointed at the tent, then all three girls turned and walked off together.

"What a great tent I got stuck in," Nadine mumbled as she shoved another chip in her mouth. "I can see I made a mistake thinking I'd be any happier here than stuck in the city with my miserable family."

Her counsellor spoke very softly as she turned and walked away. "You're probably right, Nadine. You're probably right."

Sure enough, for the first week and a half of camp, Nadine was anything but happy. None of the other kids wanted to spend any time around her. She complained about everything, often talking about how much better off she would have been at home, where she seemed to have every luxury – computer games, a hot tub, a swimming pool without "stupid rules," her own television and VCR. "I don't know how anyone could be happy at this hole-in-the-wall camp" was her first comment at every meal. It's no surprise that everyone rushed to fill up their table before Nadine came into the dining room.

I'm not sure how Nadine ended up on one of the week-long, out-of-camp trips. Maybe someone decided that at least on a trip she could only make nine other people miserable instead of the entire camp. Anyway, Nadine ended up on my canoe trip. (Oh, lucky me.) From day one, our trip had to be different because of Nadine. On most trips, you canoe with the same person every day in order to develop your ability to work as a team. On our trip, we drew numbers at the beginning of each day to see who would canoe together. I think our counsellors were smart enough to know that no one would choose to canoe with Nadine.

It's amazing how unpleasant one person can make a trip. Thanks to Nadine's complaining and her arrogant attitude, when we made camp at night everyone was a bit on edge for the first two days of the trip. But on the third day everything changed. We were in the middle of a big lake when a storm blew in from over the mountains. The wind began to stir up waves almost a metre high. Our counsellors hollered at us to keep close together and paddle for the nearest island that was downwind of us. We were more than three-quarters of the way there when a large swell washed right over Sonya and Nadine's canoe. The canoe was still upright but it was full of water. A second wave turned it upside down.

Sonya had tied all of her gear into the canoe just like we were supposed to do, but Nadine, of course, had refused to follow instructions. So, as soon as the canoe went over, all of her things fell out. Some things floated and were pushed away by the wind and waves. Other things just sank. Nadine went crazy. First she tried to dive after her boots, which were sinking; but her life jacket kept her on the surface. Then she tried to swim after her "top of the line" waterproof camera in the special canoe bag; but the wind was too strong and her clothes were creating too much drag. She couldn't catch it. She took a few futile strokes after her "Italian leather" day pack; and then she started to scream. And I mean scream. She pounded the water with her fists, kicked so hard that her shoes came off, and pulled at her own hair. I almost wanted to laugh, but then she started to sob. I've never heard anyone cry like that before and I never want to hear it again. She cried so hard she started to choke. I think all of us wondered if she would survive.

Our counsellors tried to rescue her from the water, but she was shaking and crying too hard to co-operate with them. With the storm they couldn't get her into the canoe if she wouldn't help them, and they couldn't really tow her along behind. Finally they decided that one counsellor, and the camper who was paddling with her, Camela, would stay with Nadine, while the other counsellor paddled with the rest of us the last little distance to the island.

I guess Nadine must have either calmed down or worn herself out shortly after that because we had just finished setting up our tents when the second counsellor arrived with Camela and Nadine.

It was the strangest thing. I don't think anyone remembered how much of a pain Nadine had been. Everyone rushed up to her and gave her a big hug. Everyone offered her some of their clothing. Two girls offered to zip their sleeping bags together so that all three of them could sleep in the two bags. Sonya, who had borne the brunt of some of Nadine's cruelest comments in the past, called Nadine over to sit by her on a log near the fire. While the rest of us got dinner ready, the two of them talked about how they had felt when they saw the wave coming for them, and what they thought when their boat filled up with water, and how scared they'd been when the second wave came.... They told and retold their adventure until they were the best of friends.

Nadine really changed after that. I wouldn't say she became the easiest person to get along with, but at least she tried to be part of the group. Maybe she tried to get along with people because it's easier to ask your friends if you can borrow their clothes. Maybe she pitched in to help with extra chores because it was her way of saying thank you for a sleeping bag or a candy bar. Then again, maybe she just found it easier to get along with people because now she had something in common with them.

Anyway, for the rest of the session no one ever heard her say, "I don't know how anyone could be happy here."

Jesus Teaches Us About Being Happy

In Luke 6.20-42, we find Jesus teaching his disciples some surprising lessons.[1] Read the commentaries on Jesus' teaching below, and then read the passage in your bible.

What's the matter with wealth?

Jesus said, "Woe to you who are rich, for you have received your consolation."

[1] Verses 20-22 are known as the Beatitudes. (Luke's version of the Beatitudes is a little different from the one found in Matthew 5.2-12.) The word "beatitude" comes from the Latin word for "blessed."

If being rich is such a bad thing, why do so many people buy lottery tickets hoping they'll win millions? What was Jesus talking about?

The kind of wealth Jesus warned us against is the kind that leads us to value things more than people. That kind of wealth really does bring sorrow, not joy.

Jesus tells us that if possessions are what we want, we should realize that we already have lots of them. If we rely on things to give us joy, and make getting and keeping things a priority in our lives, we're already about as happy as we're going to get.

What's so great about poverty?

Okay, so wealth that we won't share can make us unhappy and looking for wealth instead of making friends can make us unhappy. But Jesus also said, "Blessed are you who are poor." How could poverty be good?

To say that people are blessed is to say that they have been given what it takes to be truly happy. When we don't have very much, we are more likely to realize that possessions don't make people valuable or fun to be around. We are also less likely to keep away from other people – if we don't have much, we won't be worried that our things will get damaged or that being with people who don't have much will make us look bad. When we don't own a large number of things, we are more likely to develop the kinds of relationships where people share what they have and value one another for who they are.

People who do not worry about buying things or keeping them safe find it easier to build strong and loving relationships. They are more likely to "live in the kingdom of God" – that is, to live the way God wants them to live.

Isn't laughter a good thing?

Jesus said, "Blessed are you who weep now" and "Woe to you who are laughing now."

When Jesus says, "Blessed are you who weep now," he is saying that people who see that the world is not what it should be have taken the first step in living life God's way. Those who are laughing have not even noticed that there are problems that need fixing.

When we do not love enough to hurt inside when other people are hurting, our lives are shallow and our friendships have no roots. But if we share in the struggle of those who are hurting, if we are willing to love people so much that their tears become our tears, we will have the kind of loving relationships that God wants us to have. We will find true joy.

Why wouldn't I want to be popular?

Jesus said, "Blessed are you when people hate you, and when they exclude you, revile you, and defame you on account of the Son of Man...." But "woe to you when all speak well of you...."

Jesus said that we are well on our way to happiness when we have the courage to act and not react. We are blessed when we are willing to do what we believe is right even if other people tease us. When we can make our own choices even when our peers make fun of us, we have found true freedom. Real friendships grow from mutual respect and acceptance, not from doing whatever will impress the people we wish to be friends with.

"Woe to you when all speak well of you" because this may make it harder for you to do the right thing (sometimes doing the right thing makes you less popular). "Woe to you when all speak well of you" because the more you have to lose, the harder it will be for you to speak the truth.

What's wrong with revenge? Why not give 'em what they deserve?

Jesus said, "Love your enemies, do good to those who hate you, bless those who curse you, pray for those who abuse you."

Jesus tells us that the road to happiness is found by those who are strong enough to love even in the face of hate. Hate prevents a person from really being happy. Hate goes with anger and frustration, not joy. Try clenching your fists and making an angry face and then feeling really happy. That's very hard, if not impossible. In the same way, if we let hatred or a wish for revenge tie us up in knots inside, we will not be truly happy people.

People who respond to anger with anger or to hatred with hatred are reacting, not acting. They are not taking charge of their own lives; instead, they are accepting the garbage from other people's lives. People who are kind no matter how other people behave, who are generous no matter what other people choose, are really free to be themselves. They are the ones who will find true happiness.

Jesus challenges us to be the kind of people we want to be. If we want to be strong people, then we cannot sit down as soon as our load becomes a little heavy. If we want to be tough people, we cannot give up as soon as we feel a little pain. If we want to be loving people, we cannot begin to hate as soon as someone hates us. What kind of person do you want to be? What do you have to do to become that kind of person?

What happened to good old common sense?

We all know that sensible people wouldn't lend money to someone who probably wouldn't pay them back, and smart people don't keep giving to people who take and take without giving anything back.

But Jesus said, "Do good, and lend, expecting nothing in return."

Jesus tells us that our "common sense" can keep us from building loving relationships and true friendships. Real friendships are based on caring. True friends help and support each other even when they get little in return.

How can we say that we really care about someone if we only do as much for that person as he or she does for us? What would happen if parents loved their young children that way? If our friendships are like business deals, with both people trying to get just a little more than they give, we will find ourselves without friends on the day when things go wrong and we have nothing to give. Unless we share with friends who have very little, why should anyone share with us on the day when we have very little?

If we want to find true happiness, we will learn to make true friends. We will give because we care about our friends, not because we expect to get something back.

Wouldn't a little constructive criticism help some people?

Most of us find it a lot easier to criticize other people and to point out their faults than to look at our own faults and weaknesses. When things are not going well, we might think that other people are causing the problem. How many times have we said or thought, "If only so-and-so would change, I would be a lot happier"?

Jesus reminds us that when things are not going well, we need to start by looking at our own behaviour. What do we have the power to change? What parts of the "problem" do we control? If we do

what we can instead of complaining about what other people are not doing or suggesting what they could be doing, we may find that the problem is not as big as we thought.

Before we try to correct other people, we must first look at what we could do differently. Jesus says that we must take the log out of our own eye before we try to take the speck out of someone else's. We are the person with a log in our eye when we think that someone else deserves all the blame for a problem in our lives. We will be happier people if we spend less time trying to change those around us and more time learning to recognize the things in ourselves that need improvement and that we have the power to change.

Meditation

Meditate on Luke 6.20-38. As you pray, ask God to help you find the answer to this question: "What do I need to be happy?"

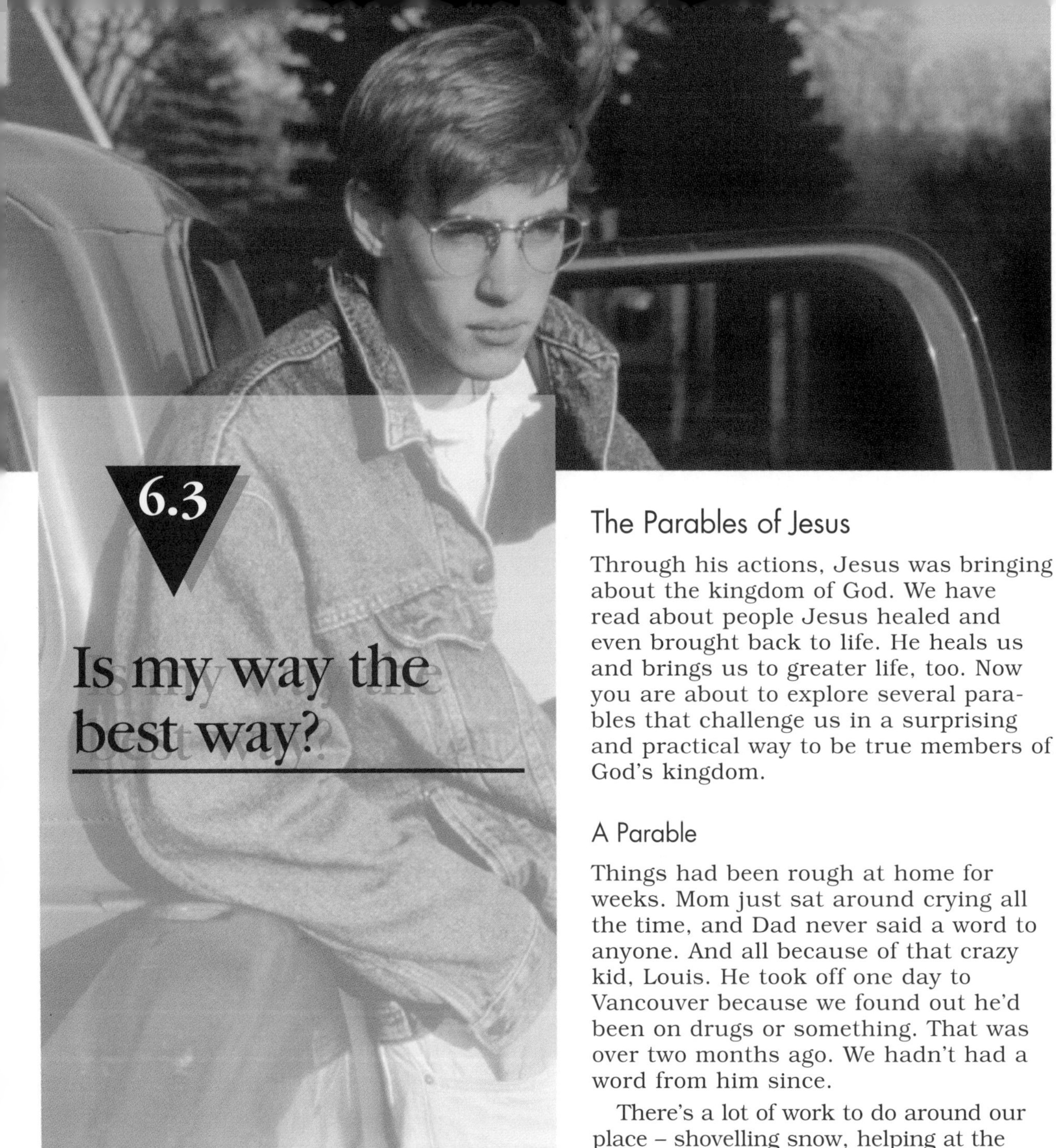

6.3

Is my way the best way?

The Parables of Jesus

Through his actions, Jesus was bringing about the kingdom of God. We have read about people Jesus healed and even brought back to life. He heals us and brings us to greater life, too. Now you are about to explore several parables that challenge us in a surprising and practical way to be true members of God's kingdom.

A Parable

Things had been rough at home for weeks. Mom just sat around crying all the time, and Dad never said a word to anyone. And all because of that crazy kid, Louis. He took off one day to Vancouver because we found out he'd been on drugs or something. That was over two months ago. We hadn't had a word from him since.

There's a lot of work to do around our place – shovelling snow, helping at the store and, on top of that, the four subjects I'm doing this semester are really heavy.

Seems like I haven't seen the gang for ages.

Then last night I came home and the whole house was lit up like a Christmas tree: cars in the driveway, music from the basement – what was going on? Mom was in the kitchen cooking up a storm, smiling and looking ten years younger. I could hear Dad laughing and joking in the basement with the neighbours.

I went downstairs and there was Louis – home! And he was wearing a new leather jacket just like the one I'd asked Mom to get me for my birthday.

"Hi, Pete," he said to me. Just like that! Just as if nothing had happened!

Dad saw me bolt upstairs again and caught up with me on the back porch. "Pete, come back," he said.

"It's not fair, Dad! I've worked like a dog, haven't seen my friends for weeks, but as soon as 'golden boy' there turns up, it's party time! And that jacket.... No, Dad!"

"Pete, you're a good boy. Your mother and I appreciate all you do, but Louis is back. We thought we'd lost him for good and now he's home. Please, Pete, we're a family. He's your brother!"

Reflection questions

1. How do you feel after hearing this story? Why?
2. What would you do if you were Pete?
3. What would you do if you were Pete's mom or dad?
4. How would you feel if you were Louis?
5. Why is Pete unhappy?
6. What would make him happy at this point?
7. What can this story help us to understand about true joy and real love?

The Labourers in the Vineyard: A Dramatic Retelling of Matthew 20.1-16

Narrator:
The kingdom of heaven is like a landowner who went out early in the morning to hire labourers for his vineyard.

Labourers (Group 1):
We are labourers who were in the marketplace looking for work for the day. The landowner told us that he had jobs for us in his vineyard.

Landowner:
I talked with the labourers about the wage I would pay them for their work.

Landowner and Labourers (Group 1):
We agreed on the usual wage for this type of work. One denarius for the day's work.

Narrator:
At about nine o'clock that same morning, the landowner went into the marketplace again.

Landowner:
I saw some poor labourers who still had not found work.

Labourers (Group 2):
He told us to go work in his vineyard. He said that he would pay us whatever was just at the end of the day.

Narrator:
The landowner went out again at noon.

Labourers (Group 3):
We were very glad when he approached us and told us that he had some work for us in his vineyard. Half a day's work is better than none at all.

Labourers (Group 4):
If you were glad to be hired at noon, imagine how we felt when he came and offered us work at 3 p.m. Perhaps we wouldn't have much to eat that night, but a few hours of work would let us bring home something.

Narrator:
At five o'clock, the landowner went into the marketplace one more time.

Landowner:
I saw people standing around doing nothing. I asked them why they were hanging around in the marketplace having done nothing all day.

Labourers (Group 5):
We told him no one had hired us. Do you know, he actually told us to go and work in his vineyard! Sundown was only an hour away. Most of us had given up hope of earning money for even a bit of bread.

Narrator:
When sundown finally came, the landowner told his manager to pay each of the labourers, beginning with those who were hired last.

Labourers (Group 5):
We came forward to receive our pay. We'd only been hired at 5 o'clock; it wouldn't be much.

Landowner: I told them that I would pay what was just.

Labourers (Group 5):
We couldn't believe it! He gave us a full day's wages. Each of us had earned enough to feed our family for another day.

Labourers (Group 1):
When we saw how much the landowner was paying those who'd only worked an hour, we got very excited. We had worked a full day – just think how much we would get!

Landowner:
I gave them the usual wage for a day's work.

Labourers (Group 1):
We were mad! Some of these others only worked for an hour. We worked for the whole day in the scorching heat. Yet you paid them as much as you paid us. You weren't being just.

Landowner:
Friends, I did you no wrong. Did you not agree with me for the usual daily wage?

Labourers (Group 1):
(*quietly*) Yes.

Landowner:
Isn't that what I paid you? Take what belongs to you and go. I choose to give to this last group the same as I give to you. Am I not allowed to do what I choose with what belongs to me? Or are you envious because I am generous?

The Lord's Prayer

Our Father,
who art in heaven,
hallowed be thy name;
thy kingdom come;
thy will be done on earth
as it is in heaven.
Give us this day our daily bread
and forgive us our trespasses
as we forgive those
who trespass against us;
and lead us not into temptation,
but deliver us from evil.
Amen.

Unit 6 Summary Statements

- The kingdom of God is not a place; it is a way of living. When we live the way God wants us to live, we are living in the kingdom of God.
- We call Jesus "Lord" because he is the one who is "in charge" of the kingdom. He makes it possible for us to share in the joy of the kingdom.
- When we call Jesus "Lord," we agree to see right and wrong the way he does.
- We can find true freedom and happiness only by living our lives according to God's way. God's way is not the way of quick, easy answers, but of genuine and patient love.
- The devil tempted Jesus to give up God's way and take a shortcut to fame and power. Jesus chose to stay faithful to God.
- True happiness is found in building loving relationships.
- If we wish to live in the kingdom of God, we must first love God and other people. We must not let a desire for possessions, popularity or power take over our lives.
- Parables challenge us to think in new ways and to look at our own attitudes and actions in new ways.
- Parables draw us into the mystery of the kingdom of God, a mystery that is greater than the human mind can understand.
- The kingdom of God is not about competing with each other. It is about unity and sharing in joy.
- Every action I take for God's kingdom will have an effect that goes far beyond me.
- When we pray the Lord's Prayer, we show both our wish to live according to God's way and our need for God's help to live according to God's way.

Key Terms

kingdom of God
fasting
abstinence
temptations
true happiness
Beatitudes
parable
the Lord's Prayer

Unit 7

We believe in Jesus...who was conceived by the power of the Holy Spirit and born of the Virgin Mary.

7.1

Why is everybody always picking on me?

"Why am I always chosen for things like this?"

> "Lord, I know we're the chosen people; but once in a while couldn't you choose someone else?"
> *Tevye in Fiddler on the Roof*
>
> "So if anyone is in Christ, there is a new creation: everything old has passed away; see, everything has become new!"
> *2 Corinthians 5.17*
>
> "We know that all things work together for good for those who love God...."
> *Romans 8.28*

Far from Home

It was nighttime. There was plenty of movement in the camp as over a hundred teenage boys, all of whom had been taken by force from their homes by the army, selected places to sleep and made those places as comfortable as possible. Before stretching out for the night, most of the boys wandered a little way from the camp to relieve themselves in the privacy of the trees. The guards did not notice that some of the boys who went into the woods did not return. Perhaps they did not suspect that young boys far from home would venture off into the dense forest, filled with unknown dangers, in the middle of the night. But many of the boys felt that they had nothing to lose. Thirteen-year-old Rovino was among them.

The boys hid in the forest for the rest of the night and all the next day. When night came again they began a long, uncertain journey toward the Kenyan border. Water was scarce; food was scarce; and military patrols could be anywhere. The boys watched many of their friends die along the way. Only a fraction of those who had escaped the military made it to the border.

Of that fraction, only a fraction have found a life beyond the refugee camps.

Rovino is one of the lucky ones. He's now in high school in Canada, and in a year or two he will be attending university. Rovino is grateful. He is alive. He doesn't have to worry about starving or about being shot. He will never be forced to aim a rifle at those he loves. But his life in Canada is still not easy. He is far from his home. It's been a long time since he saw his family or the friends he grew up with; and there is no guarantee that he'll ever see them again. Furthermore, although he is very smart, people often discount him because his English is not yet perfect. There are even those who hate him just because he wasn't born in Canada.

Some people might give up. There were times when Rovino wanted to, but his faith is strong. He believes that "in Christ everything becomes new" and "all things work together for good for those who love God." For Rovino, the pain of his past has become strength for the present. When he thinks that things are impossible, he remembers all of the "impossible" things God has helped him do, and all of the bad things that God used for good, and he finds the strength and courage to go on. He knows that for each awful thing he has been through, he has also been given a new and wonderful opportunity. He clings to the good things. Those are gifts from God.

Rovino loves people in both Canada and Sudan. He has friends in Canada who are aware of and offer help to people in Sudan whom they "know" through Rovino's stories. He has friends in Sudan who pray for people in Canada because of their relationship to Rovino. Through Rovino, and many others like him, people in each place have developed a relationship with the people in the other. Slowly but surely, love will replace fear. Slowly but surely, the desire to understand will replace the wish to ignore or condemn.

Rovino has co-operated with God by being willing to love the people around him regardless of their background. Rovino has co-operated with God in his willingness to struggle for life no matter how hopeless things seem. God's plan for creation, that all people should be one, is a little closer to completion because of Rovino.

What's the Point?

Collin's dad died when Collin was halfway through Grade 7. His mom pulled all of the kids out of school in Manitoba and they headed east to where his grandparents lived.

"Mom said we needed to be around family. I didn't care. When they told me my dad died, a noise started in the back of my head, like a smoke alarm that just wouldn't stop. I couldn't cry. I couldn't talk. Nothing seemed to matter, just that noise that kept going and going." That's how Collin remembers this time in his life.

"I hated God and everything to do with God. Why didn't God work a miracle? I hated life. It all seemed so pointless. I did just about every stupid thing a kid can do, but nothing took the pain away. I was empty. Then I met some little kids who were worse off than me. I had a mom who, despite everything, loved me. Their mom had...well...let's just say their mom hadn't been very loving. I cried for those kids. They were so little, only eight and ten; I cried for them like I could never cry for myself. There had to be a way I could make their life better. God help me. God.... I prayed. I actually prayed."

Collin's an adult now. He works in a home for boys who have been in trouble. Most of the kids there have been abused or abandoned. In Collin, many of the boys have found someone who cares about them and understands.

"Everything has become new." Collin's pain has helped him reach out to those who are hurting. Because of Collin, a few more kids know that there's more to the world than violence. Collin's dad's heart attack wasn't a good thing, but God works good in all things if we will co-operate with God. That heart attack changed a lot of boys' lives for the better.

Don't Wreck My Life!

Susan's mom is getting married again. The man she's marrying has two kids who live with him. Susan is not happy. Everything's going to change! Her mom won't spend as much time with her anymore. She'll have to share things with a "brother" and "sister" she doesn't really know. Some other adult will think he has a right to tell her what to do. It's going to be awful.

Susan has cried, screamed and even threatened to leave home, but it hasn't changed anything. The wedding is getting very close.

"Kip, what am I going to do?" Susan was at her friend Kip's house, where she'd spent most of her time lately.

"Susan, give it up. Your mom's going to get married. You can make it the worst experience of your life or you can make the best of it. My dad got remarried two years ago. I kind of like having a stepbrother; at least when something goes wrong it's not automatically my fault. I don't pretend that my dad's marriage is the greatest thing that ever happened to me. But it really wasn't bad once I stopped screaming at everyone all the time and picking fights every chance I got."

"What made you stop?"

"One day, Dad sat down with me. He said, 'Listen, Kip, I love you now and I've always loved you, but you're making it pretty impossible for love to get through to you right now. I've remarried and that's all there is to it. If you want to spend your life wishing for the past, that's your business, but it won't bring the past back. I'd suggest that you look for some good in the present. If nothing else, other people will like being around you more.' It hurt when he said that. I realized that I wasn't much fun to be around when all I was doing was complaining. I made this corny little promise to myself to say one nice thing about my stepmother every day. Believe it or not, it worked. I still don't think she's Mrs. Wonderful, but at least my stomach doesn't go into knots every time I think of her. And you know what else? I find that I don't get so mad about other things I can't change now either. I'm a lot more relaxed about life. Don't tell my dad this, but I may actually be a better person."

"Oh, Kip, why did you have to say that! I don't want to like my stepdad! But I suppose I am a bit tired of being miserable, and I know my friends are tired of it."

So much of how life goes depends on the attitude we take toward life. If we believe that "everything old becomes new" and "all things work for good for those who love God," even the hardest situations can bring about unexpected good. God is full of wonderful surprises.

Grace

Grace is taking part in God's own life. It is a gift from God. Grace helps us to want what God wants and to respond to the call to live as God's children.

Rovino, Collin, Kip and Susan were all given the ability to see life from a whole new point of view. All of them had a change of heart that let them see something good in a hard situation. They all experienced God's grace. Their lives didn't become easy. Their pain did not go away. But they still found the courage and the desire to work with God to make something new.

Grace invites us to respond, but it does not make us respond. God made it possible for Susan, Kip, Collin and Rovino to bring good out of a bad situation, but each of them was always free to ignore God and accept pain and misery.

What Mary Might Tell Us

My name is Mary. I live in a town in Galilee called Nazareth. I have just heard the news that God has chosen me to be the mother of the Messiah. Me, Mary! I was afraid when I first heard the news. I didn't think that I was ready to have a child. What's worse, I'm not married. If people think I slept with someone who was not my husband, I could be stoned to death. I hope God speaks to Joseph!

Joseph is the man I am engaged to. In my culture it's frowned upon if a woman sleeps with her fiancé before they are married, but at least if it's her fiancé she won't be put to death. If Joseph is willing to accept this baby as his own, people may question our behaviour but my life will be spared. The problem, of course, is that Joseph knows that this child can't be his. He and I haven't slept together. If he thinks that I have brought shame to him and makes a public statement that this is not his baby, I'll be executed. There is a risk.

But I'm a faithful Jew. I know that all life belongs to God. If God wants me to bear the Son of God, that is what I will do. I must trust that God will do what is best for me as long as I am willing to co-operate with God. Surely all things work for good for those who love God.

I told the angel: "I am a servant of the Lord; let it be with me according to your word." I could go into hiding now, or I could go and visit my cousin Elizabeth. She too has been blessed by God.

• • • • •

Well, I went to see Elizabeth. As soon as I arrived, she knew that God had blessed me. She knew that the baby I was carrying was to be the Messiah. I knew that the world was changing; we would never be able to look at things in quite the same way.

I think that most of us had always imagined that the Messiah would be rich and powerful. Surely no one thought that he would be born as a poor baby, his mother an unknown Jewish girl. God's idea of power and greatness is clearly quite different from ours! That's going to make some people very unhappy.

We have two real choices now. We can complain and be afraid because the world that we knew is passing away and we have no guarantees for the future. Or we can get excited about the possibilities of a world where love and service will be more important than money or position. I'm excited! God has given those of us who felt powerless a whole new reason to hope.

Speaking of hope, I'm happy to say that my prayers have been answered. God has spoken with Joseph. Joseph agreed to take me as his wife and accept this child as his own son. That must have been a pretty hard decision for him. It takes a lot of courage to risk looking foolish in order to do what is right. Joseph also believes that if we serve God, even in hard times, God will make what is old and crumbling new and strong.

I'm glad that Joseph is willing to rely on God in this whole thing. As if he didn't already have enough on his mind, Joseph has found out that we must go to Bethlehem for some type of census. I'm just trusting that there is a reason for all of this, and that good that I cannot even imagine will come out of it if I keep my faith in God.

• • • • •

Well, we made it to Bethlehem, but there are so many people here, we couldn't find a room at an inn. It's hard to believe that the Son of God's first bed should be a manger, but that's all there was. A few hours after Jesus was born, shepherds from nearby came to see him. They said that they had been sent by an angel of God. Maybe the Son of God was born in such a simple place so that even shepherds would be able to come to give him honour.

Everything that has happened to us has resulted in unexpected blessings. It hasn't always been easy, but God has been with us. I really do believe that people are invited to work with God to give shape to creation and make new what is old. We experience grace when we are willing to let go of the old and accept the new that God desires.

Two Catholic teachings that are often confused:

The virgin birth: Mary was a virgin when Jesus was born. Jesus does not have a biological human father. Joseph was Jesus' adoptive father. God is Jesus' true father. That is why we say in the Creed that Jesus was "conceived by the power of the Holy Spirit and born of the Virgin Mary." The virgin birth is a reminder of the truth of the Angel Gabriel's words: "Nothing will be impossible with God."

The Immaculate Conception: Mary was sustained by divine grace throughout her life. From the moment she was conceived, her heart was with God and she found the strength and the courage to live as God wanted her to live.

When we pray the Hail Mary, we say that Mary is "full of grace." We celebrate the fact that she believed that God's way was always the best way, even if people could not understand it. Mary trusted in God's plan for creation. She ordered her life according to the will of God, not according to fear or selfishness.

Whenever you want to ask, "Why's everybody always picking on me?" try praying the Hail Mary. In Mary you will find someone who really understands.

Hail Mary

Hail, Mary, full of grace,
the Lord is with you;
blessed are you among women,
and blessed is the fruit of your
womb, Jesus.

Holy Mary, mother of God,
pray for us sinners
now and at the hour of our death.
Amen.

7.2 Who understands me?

"Just Like Me"

A priest who spent a few years working in a small community in the West tells this story:

Most of the people in this community were of European descent. However, there was one family, originally from Japan, who moved into the community a few years after I did. They had a son in high school and a daughter in Grade 1. I was the principal of the elementary school at the time. I remember the little girl, Saiko, quite clearly. She seemed overwhelmed by the school, by the noise and the commotion and the apparent lack of order. She chose a desk right against the wall and for the first few weeks of school she left that desk only if she absolutely had to. As time went on, Saiko made friends with some of the other girls in the class. She would play or talk quietly with them when she was on the playground. In the classroom, however, she rarely spoke and even then she never spoke above a whisper.

Saiko's teacher was worried about her, and I was a bit concerned myself. But Saiko's parents assured us that everything was fine. They laughed when we said she didn't talk. "She talks non-stop from the moment school ends until she goes to bed," her mother said. "Just ask her brother."

In January, the Grade 1 teacher had to leave the school for family reasons. We hired another teacher, a young Japanese woman who had just completed her teacher training. I'll never forget the day I took her in to introduce her to the Grade 1 class. I did not have a chance to say more than, "This is your new teacher, Miss..." when Saiko was out of her seat, running toward the front of the class.

"She's just like me!" the little girl yelled as she hugged the new teacher around the legs.

From that day forward Saiko seemed like a totally different person, more like the child her parents had described. I rarely saw her when she wasn't talking or laugh-

At the foot of Mt. Sinai

ing. The one day when I did see her sitting by herself on the playground, I could barely keep a straight face as she explained to me why she wasn't playing with everyone else: "I have to spend some time being quiet because I wouldn't stop talking in class."

The wonder of the Incarnation is that God was willing to become "just like us." (The term "Incarnation" means that God became human without ceasing to be God.) Because God became human, we can now know God better and we can also know ourselves better. In Jesus we see God, who can completely understand the struggles that human beings go through in their daily lives. Like Saiko, we can speak without fear because we trust that we will be understood. In Jesus, we also see the kind of person each of us is called to be. In Jesus we see the potential for love and compassion that is in all people. In Jesus we have a model to follow when we face tough situations.

If we are going to be take comfort from the fact that Jesus can understand us, and if we are going to see Jesus as a model for us, we must first get to know Jesus as a human being. We must learn a little about where he grew up, a little about the important issues of his day, and a little about the struggles he had to face. Jesus' life was both like and unlike our own.

I. Where Jesus Lived: The Land and Its People

At the southeast corner of the Mediterranean Sea lies a land of rocky hills and barren desert, green valleys and ancient cities, winter rain and burning summer sun.

You can drive all the way across this tiny land in a couple of hours. As you drive east from the Mediterranean, you go across a flat coastal plain with good useable land – but in some places it is only a few hundred metres wide. Then you start climbing a twisty road through rocky hills, for the central part of this land is a long chain of rather low mountains. After more than 60 kilometres through these hills, the road turns downward into the valley of the Jordan River.

The whole country is no more than 100 kilometres across. From north to south, it is about 400 kilometres.

But even though this country is very small, some of the greatest peoples who ever lived have come from this place.

Two different groups of people call this land home. People of Arabic heritage have lived here for centuries. People of Jewish heritage have also lived here for centuries. Today this land is divided between these two groups.

At the time of Jesus, the land was made up of three districts (like the way Canada is made up of provinces and territories). Their names are still used today: Judea, Samaria and Galilee.

Judea

The southern district is called Judea. Judea is mostly desert – but not a desert of endless sand like the Sahara. The Judean desert is made of rocky hills and

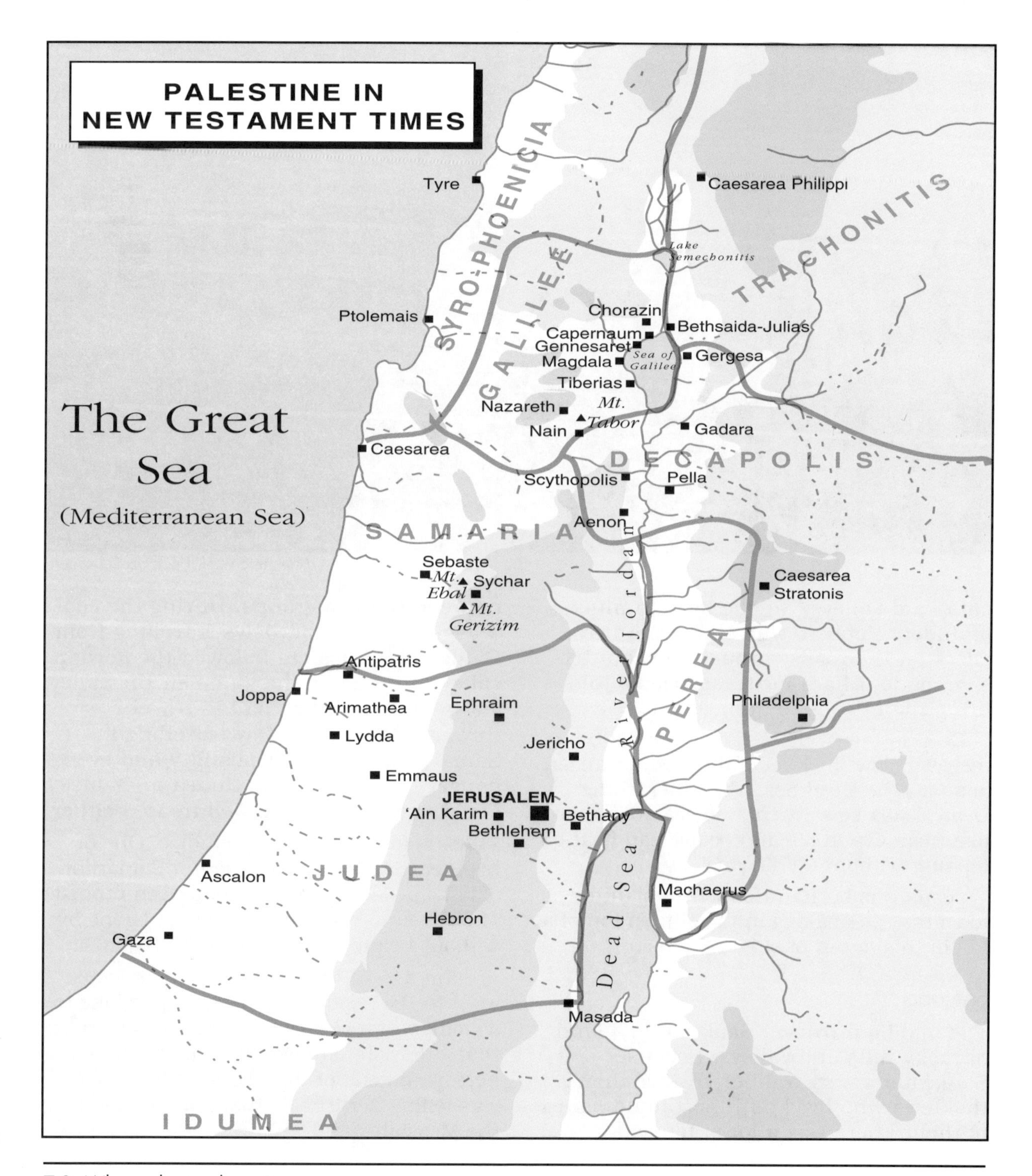
PALESTINE IN
NEW TESTAMENT TIMES
The Great
Sea
(Mediterranean Sea)
Tyre
Caesarea Philippi
SYRO-PHOENICIA
GALILEE
Lake
Semechonitis
TRACHONITIS
Ptolemais
Chorazin
Bethsaida-Julias
Capernaum
Gennesaret
Sea of
Galilee
Gergesa
Magdala
Tiberias
Nazareth
Mt.
Tabor
Nain
Gadara
Caesarea
DECAPOLIS
Scythopolis
Pella
Aenon
SAMARIA
Sebaste
Mt.
Ebal
Sychar
Mt.
Gerizim
Caesarea
Stratonis
River Jordan
PEREA
Antipatris
Joppa
Arimathea
Ephraim
Philadelphia
Lydda
Jericho
Emmaus
JERUSALEM
'Ain Karim
Bethany
Bethlehem
Ascalon
JUDEA
Dead Sea
Machaerus
Hebron
Gaza
Masada
IDUMEA

Shepherds' fields outside Bethlehem

cliffs and valleys. No one lived in much of Judea. Robbers who stole from travellers on the roads through the countryside made it hard for tradespeople to bring their goods to Jerusalem.

Deep in one of those hot valleys, 400 metres below the level of the Mediterranean Sea, lies the Dead Sea. The water in the Dead Sea is so salty that no sea animal or plant can live in it – and people can float on top of it without even trying.

Jesus was born in Bethlehem of Judea, a town that sits baking in the sun on top of a hill in this desert of stone.

Samaria

The middle province, Samaria, is a land of rocky hills and valleys. Because Samaritans were a different race than the Jews who lived both north and south of them, there was a lot of tension between the two groups. During the cool seasons of the year, Jews travelling from Galilee to Jerusalem followed the Jordan valley, but during the summer, the valley got too hot and they had to travel through Samaria. A Jew travelling in Samaria could expect hostility and even danger. A Samaritan in Judea or Galilee could not expect to be well treated either.

Jesus fought against prejudice. One of his greatest stories was about a Samaritan who helped someone who had been robbed after several "religious" people had gone by without helping (see Luke 10.30-37).

John 4.7-26 tells of a time when Jesus went to the region of Samaria and spoke to a woman at a well there. She was surprised that a Jewish man would even speak to her; by the end of their conversation, she was telling her friends that she had found the Messiah.

Galilee

After his family left Bethlehem when he was only a baby, Jesus lived most of his life in the northern province, Galilee. The rocky hillsides there are covered with grass and flowers in the spring, but they are dry in the hot summer and nothing grows. (There are other hillsides and valleys where food can be grown.)

The Sea of Galilee (also called the Sea of Tiberias and the Lake of Gennesaret) is a small freshwater lake fed by the winter rains in the hills above it. The Jordan River flows south from the Sea of Galilee to the Dead Sea. In the winter and spring, a strong east wind known as the Sharkiyeh sometimes blows across the lake. This wind is feared by fishermen even today. It often begins without warning; it can stir up large waves and make it impossible to row or sail.

Some Galileans (like Peter and Andrew, James and John) were fishermen who made their living on that rather small lake called the Sea of Galilee. Some, like Jesus, were craftspeople in little towns such as Nazareth and Capernaum. Some Galileans worked as farmers, caring for herds or growing crops where the land was good enough.

Most of the people who lived in Galilee 2000 years ago were poor and not very well educated. Mothers and fathers often saw several of their children die, because no one knew how to cure childhood diseases. In fact, many mothers died young themselves, either because of problems in childbirth or because they had to work so hard just to keep themselves and their families alive.

Most marriages were arranged when people were quite young and took place when the bride was old enough to have children. Most men married between the ages of 18 and 24; their bride was often between 12 and 14. Many people not only married young, they often died at a young age, too. The average life expectancy in Jesus' time was 22 years! (Averages don't tell the whole story. Say there are five children in a family. If three of them die as children – ages 1, 2 and 10 – and two live to be adults who die at ages 42 and 55, their average life expectancy is 22 – and yet none of them died anywhere near the age of 22.)

Fishers on the Sea of Galilee

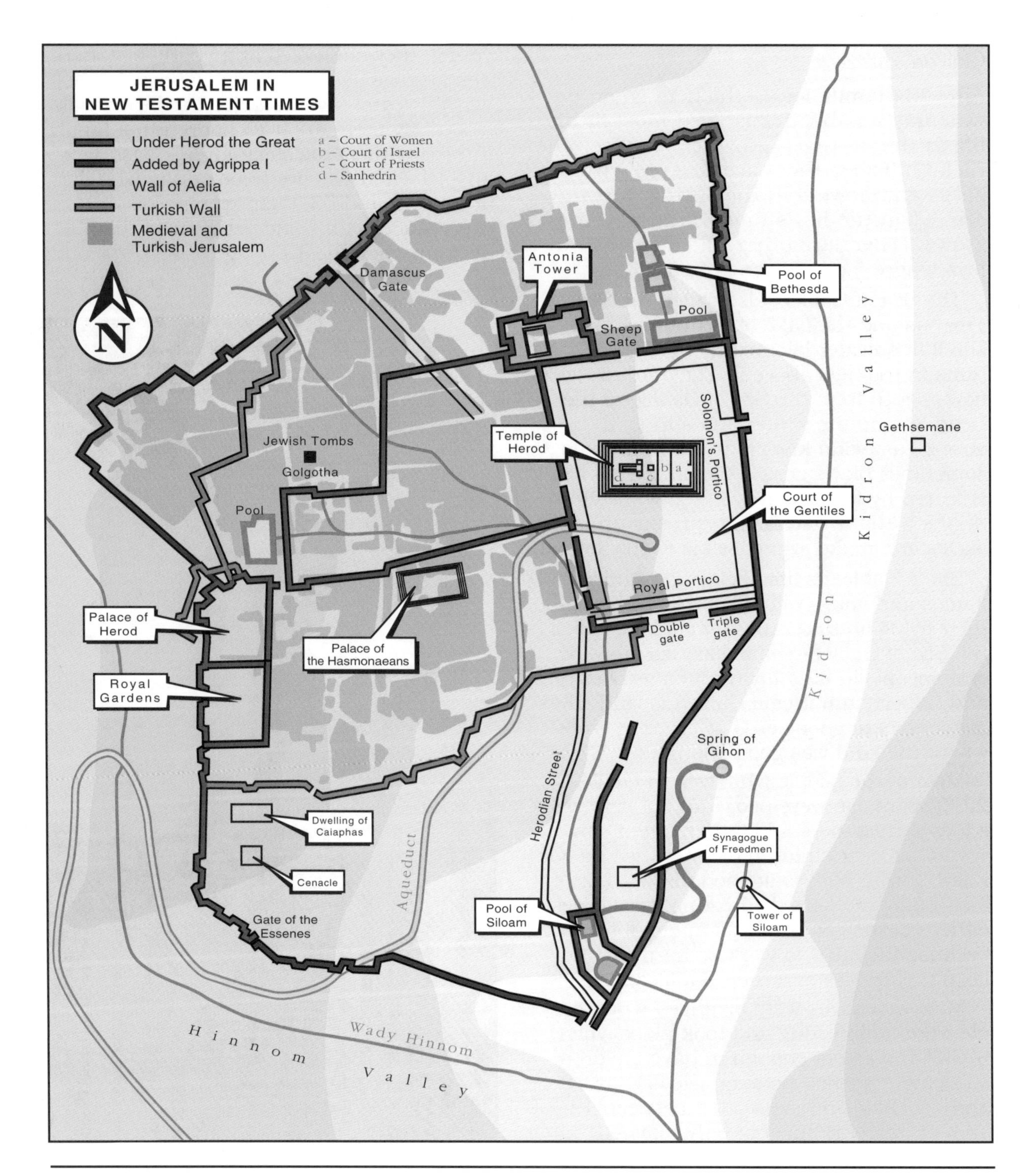

 We believe in Jesus...who was conceived by the power of the Holy Spirit and born of the Virgin Mary.

City of Jerusalem (in the district of Judea)

The capital city of the country in Jesus' time was Jerusalem. It was built as a fortress in the days of King David, a thousand years before Jesus lived. Jerusalem was a beautiful city, set on a rocky hill in the region of Judea, about 30 kilometres from the north end of the Dead Sea.

Jerusalem was the centre of Jewish culture and of the Jewish religion. There was only one Temple in the whole country, and it was in Jerusalem. Every day in the Temple, priests offered animal sacrifices in praise of God. Jewish people from all around the Mediterranean Sea came to Jerusalem for the high holy days, the great religious festivals.

A street in old Jerusalem

The Temple was not only a place where sacrifices were offered. It was also understood to be where God lived. God promised King David that David's son, Solomon, would build a house where God would always be present. This "house" was the Temple. Jews travelled from far away to visit the Temple because God was there in a very special way.

For good reason, the people of Jerusalem were proud of their city, their traditions and their importance. It was hard for them to accept that a poor smalltown craftsman, Jesus of Nazareth, was sent by God to change those traditions and to proclaim the coming of God's kingdom.

It was in the city of Jerusalem that Jesus was killed.

II. Why Were the Romans in Jesus' Homeland? And Who Was King Herod?

Two thousand years ago, Rome was the centre of a great civilization. There were a lot of good things about this society – and a lot of bad things, too. On the good side, the Romans had one of the greatest systems of law ever. They built excellent roads that joined communities together across thousands of kilometres. Because their rule was so strong, they gave people a long time of freedom from war (the *Pax Romana* – the Roman Peace) in all the vast lands they controlled. On the bad side, because they had the strongest army in the world, they felt free to march into other countries and take over.

The Romans would go into an area like Jesus' homeland and say that they were to be the government. They would increase

Herod the Great

the taxes (keeping the money for themselves) and deal cruelly with anyone who got angry enough to oppose them.

The Romans made a law that they were the only ones who could legally execute a criminal. That is why Jesus was killed by Roman soldiers under the orders of a Roman governor.

King Herod "the Great" came not from the royal family of Israel (the family of King David), but from a desert tribe that lived in a region of the south called Idumea. He got the Romans to declare him king by saying, "I'll do everything you Romans ask me to do if you'll let me rule as king of the Jews." He was only a "puppet" of the Caesar or Emperor, but he was very rich. The Jewish people hated him for co-operating with the enemy, for the Jews lived in fear of the Romans.

This King Herod was alive when Jesus was born. He liked to be in charge of great building projects, like palaces and stadiums. He even had a beautiful new Temple built in Jerusalem. But he was a suspicious man. He was always on guard against anyone who might threaten his power. Herod killed anyone he thought might be a threat to him. (He even had his wife and three of his sons killed.) That is why he ordered all infants in Bethlehem to be killed – because people said that one of them might become a king. (See Matthew 2.16.)

Herod died shortly after the birth of Jesus. His kingdom was divided among three of his sons. (They are called *tetrarchs*, meaning minor princes, in the gospels.) One of his sons was also named Herod; he was the tetrarch of Galilee, where Jesus lived. He happened to be in Jerusalem at the time of Jesus' arrest, so Pontius Pilate, the Roman governor of the area, sent Jesus over to him for trial (see Luke 23.6-16). Another of the tetrarchs was called Philip. John the Baptist was killed because he preached against Herod's marriage to Philip's former wife.

The Roman troops in Palestine became more and more brutal over time, and showed less and less respect for the Jewish religious practices. In 62 CE, the Roman governor of Jerusalem stole money from the Temple treasury. When this happened, some of the Jews went begging on behalf of the "poor governor." The governor was furious; he let his troops do whatever they wished in the city. The Jewish people fought back. For a short time, they got control of Jerusalem again. Then, in 70 CE, things got really bad. During the week of Passover, Roman soldiers attacked Jerusalem. The Jewish people both in and outside of Jerusalem fought bravely, but the Roman forces were too strong. The Romans wrecked most of the Jewish towns, killing thousands of people, and drove the Jewish people out of their homeland. By 73 CE, the fight had ended. The Jews became citizens of other countries, where they lived, worked and often suffered.

One very important event took place during the Roman victory of the year 70. The famous Temple of Jerusalem, which had just been finished, was smashed to pieces, as Jesus had foretold. It has never been rebuilt.

III. Jewish Responses to the Roman Occupation

Jesus was a Jew. So were all his friends. So were most of his enemies. Jesus went to the synagogue on the Sabbath day all his life. (The Jewish Sabbath begins at sundown on Friday and ends at sundown on Saturday.) He observed the Law of Moses. He went to the Temple in Jerusalem from time to time.

The Jewish people at the time of Jesus were struggling with the problems that the Romans were causing in their community and in their faith. Different groups of Jews responded to the Roman occupation in different ways. Jesus did not really fit into any of these groups.

Some Jews, including many of the Sadducees, believed that the only way for the Jewish people to survive was to co-operate with the Romans. They did not give up their faith but they did let it be shaped by the culture of their day. Many in this group worked in the Roman political system. They tried to smooth over some of the tensions between the Romans and those who didn't like having them around. These Jews did not like Jesus because they liked the way things were and he challenged that. They were also afraid of what might happen if the number of Jesus' followers grew too large and the Romans saw them as a threat.

Other people, including most of the pharisees, believed that Jews would only be able to survive and stay faithful to their God if they carefully observed every Jewish law and avoided those who did not follow Jewish laws, including the Romans. These Jews believed that the Law was the greatest gift God had ever given people. Anyone who ignored one law was showing disrespect for all of God's laws and therefore for God. This group was afraid that Jesus would weaken the Jewish law and the people's relationship with God. Jesus aimed many of his words and stories at this group. He tried to make them understand that God's law is more than words and rules; God's law is an attitude toward life.

Ruins of synagogue in Capernaum

Finally, many Jews believed that the Romans had no right to occupy Israel. They believed that the Roman occupation went against what God wanted. They felt that only God had a right to be king and to be called "lord." Anyone who followed the Roman emperor, paid Roman taxes or in any way accepted Roman rule was breaking the first commandment, which said that people could have no other Lord than God. These Jews believed that good Jews should get together to get rid of the Romans by force. They were not pleased when Jesus told them to love their enemies.

God Understands

The oldest passage of the New Testament may be the passage known as the Philippians' hymn. In his letter to the people in Philippi, St. Paul quotes a poem that may have been used in the earliest Christian celebrations:

"Let the same mind be in you that was in Christ Jesus,
who, though he was in the form of God,
did not regard equality with God
as something to be exploited,
but emptied himself,
taking the form of a slave,
being born in human likeness.
And being found in human form,
he humbled himself
and became obedient to the point of death –
even death on a cross.

Therefore God also highly exalted him
and gave him the name that is above every name...."

Philippians 2.6-9

Paul reminds us that Jesus accepted all of what it is to be human, including human weaknesses, limits and struggles. If Jesus was willing to accept the fact that as a human being he could not do everything, why should we be ashamed when we cannot do everything?

Jesus could not change all of the people he met. He could not convince everyone that his ideas were good. He could not teach everyone the importance and the power of love. In fact, so many people rejected Jesus and saw his message as a threat that he was executed. By human standards, Jesus failed.

It is human to fail sometimes; that's one of the things that Jesus taught us when he accepted "even death on a cross." He also taught us that if we live our lives as honestly as we can, in love and faith, God will

Doogie Dogma *(Catechism #472)*

IN HIS IMAGE

Who are the people in the painting within the Divine Person? They were chosen at random, Mr. Zdinak tells us, and include several of the members of his own family (three sons, a daughter, and Mrs. Zdinak!) as well as world-renowned celebrities. Some of the better-known people are:

1 Dr. Jonas Salk
2 Senator Robert F. Kennedy
3 Ex-Governor of N.Y. State Averell Harriman
4 Mahatma Gandi
5 President John F. Kennedy
6 Pope John XXIII
7 Dr. Martin Luther King
8 Bishop Fulton J. Sheen
9 Pope Paul VI
10 Pope Pius XII
11 Henry Luce
12 Alexander Graham Bell

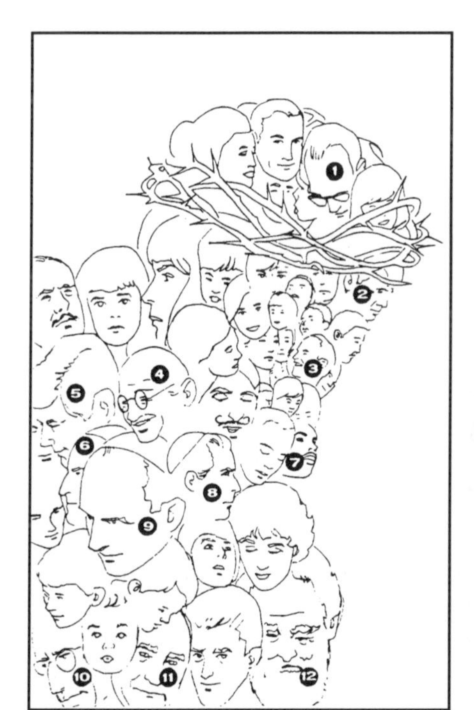

"On that day you will know that I am ... in you."
John 14.20

turn even our failures into something good. God understands our struggles. God, in the person of Jesus, has gone through the same struggles. God knows all about human success and failure, and God values and loves us whether we succeed or fail!

Sometimes we listen to the things we are supposed to do as Christians and we think, "That's impossible. Loving one's enemies might be a nice idea, but it's not practical. If I share what I have with those who aren't even grateful, if I am kind to people who will just walk all over me, I'll be nothing but a failure. People will laugh at me. God just doesn't know how hard this is." But God does know. The crowd around the cross laughed at Jesus. People Jesus grew up with made fun of him. People he had called friends abandoned him. People he had helped called for his death. Yet according to God's standards, no one has ever been as big a success as Jesus.

Reflection questions

1. How was Jesus' death on the cross a failure? How was it a success?
2. In what ways are we called to be like Jesus?
3. What is significant about the fact that Jesus is both fully human and fully God?

Jean Vanier

Life really changes if we discover the beauty of people in their weakness....

Jean Vanier

Jean Vanier, the son of the former Governor General of Canada, resigned his commission in the Royal Canadian Navy and went to France to work in a students' community. In 1964, Jean made his home with mentally handicapped adults, and so began the first l'Arche (meaning "Ark") community. To this day he has taken these mentally handicapped people for his family. Hundreds of l'Arche communities, in which certain people have chosen to share their lives with the mentally handicapped, have been set up around the world. We wrote a letter to Jean Vanier asking him to share his story with us. Here is part of his reply:

Dear Friends.

...it would be most important and truthful to write about what people with a mental handicap have taught me, the gifts they bring to our world and to the Church. For if we are living with handicapped people, it is not because we are "good people," but rather because mentally handicapped people are "good" and have something special to teach us. Unfortunately, so many people do not realize this, that they are the ones leading us to greater humility and deeper understanding of Jesus and of his message in the gospels. They are the ones who help us discover our human dignity. So if you want to write about us, you will have to write about the beauty of people who have a mental handicap and their generosity in welcoming us.

And again, what is important for teenagers to discover is not what Jean Vanier or Mme. Vanier have done, but rather the beauty, power, strength that are hidden in the heart of the weak. Most people reject those who are weak. They also reject their own weakness. But life really changes if we discover the beauty of people in their weakness and the presence of God hidden in them.

May God bless you,
Jean Vanier

Unit 7 Summary Statements

- Jesus was conceived through the initiative of God with human co-operation. Part of the mystery of salvation is that God works with us.
- Grace is a gift from God. Grace helps us to want what God wants and to respond to the call to live as God's children.
- Mary is an example of one who hears the word of God and responds to it with her whole heart.
- The term "virgin birth" means that Mary was a virgin when Jesus was born. Jesus does not have a biological human father.
- The term "Immaculate Conception" means that Mary was sustained by divine grace throughout her life. From the moment she was conceived, her heart was with God.
- Jesus is fully human and fully divine – from the moment of his conception for all eternity.
- Jesus is our model of holiness. He shows that true holiness does not go against human nature but is the purest expression of it.
- As we learn more about when and where Jesus lived, we can identify more with his humanity and learn to see how his life can be a model for our own.
- Because of the Incarnation, we can be sure that God understands what it is to be human. Jesus experienced human limitations and potential.
- The term "Incarnation" means that the Son of God became human and accepted all of the limitations of being human, but he never stopped being God.
- During the time of Jesus, the Romans occupied the land of Israel. Jewish responses to the Roman occupation were varied. Some Jews believed it was best to co-operate with the Romans. Others thought Jews should avoid the Romans as much as possible. Still others believed the Jews should revolt against the Romans.
- At the time of Jesus, the land of Israel was divided into three districts: Judea, Samaria and Galilee. Jesus was born in and died in Judea. He lived most of his life in Galilee.

Key Terms

grace
the virgin birth
the Hail Mary
Incarnation
Judea
Galilee
Samaria
Jerusalem
Herod
the Roman occupation
the Immaculate Conception

Unit 8

He suffered under Pontius Pilate, was crucified, died and was buried. He descended to the dead.

8.1 What risks are worth taking ?

Should I Have Kept Quiet?

It happened on a school trip. This trip was a really big deal. Our school board had never before allowed kids our age to go away overnight, and we were to be gone for a whole week. Our teachers wanted everything to go well. Weeks before the trip, they sat us all down and explained how important it was that we follow every rule. If anything went wrong on this trip we would spoil things for all the grades that followed us.

There had already been some problems with drinking and drugs in our school. A lot of parents were worried about what might happen if any of the kids brought stuff with them on the trip. So our teachers made one rule even stricter than all the others: anyone caught with illegal drugs or alcohol would be kicked out of our school. There would be no exceptions. Before we could go on the trip we had to sign forms that said we understood the rule. Our parents had to sign similar forms.

The fourth day of the trip was one of those really humid days when all smells seem really strong. The teacher in charge of the trip went into one of the dormitory rooms to talk with a couple of the kids. When he sat down on a chair near the end of one of the beds, he smelled stale beer. He looked at the blanket that was folded at the end of the bed and saw that it had a stain on it. When he picked it up, the beer smell was even stronger. He unfolded the blanket. It seemed as if someone who had been drinking had gotten sick on the blanket and had wiped it clean but not washed it.

Four kids were sharing that room. All of them swore that they had not drunk any alcohol on the trip. Three of the kids were the kind who never really get into trouble. Anyway, they had been up late in the common lounge playing cards every night. The fourth kid was someone who often boasted about drinking even when teachers were within earshot. Two nights earlier, he had gone to his room early, claiming that he didn't feel very well. The beer-stained blanket was at the end of his bed.

The teacher didn't need any more information. "That's it, Simon! You're out of here. Pack your bags now. We'll call your parents and tell them to meet the next bus."

"But I wasn't drinking!"

"Simon, I don't want to hear one of your lines. You've gone too far this time." Mr. Hayward was one of those teachers who's not afraid of enforcing rules. We'd often heard him complain that other teachers were inconsistent; they threatened kids with all kinds of punishments but they never followed through. He wasn't like that. As far as Mr. Hayward was concerned, Simon had known the rule, he had broken it, and now he would pay for it.

"But sir, I wasn't drinking."

"Simon, you've lied one time too many. You're not going to tell me that this blanket smelled like this all week and you never said anything."

"I never noticed the smell. I've only used the blanket to cover the bottom half of me. It hasn't been near my face."

"Simon, as soon as you sit near the bed you can smell the blanket. You don't need to put it by your face. Now pack."

I wasn't one of the people staying in the room. I was just there playing cards. Plus I don't like Simon. So who knows why I decided to say anything. Maybe it was just that I believe in honesty and fairness. Anyway, I opened my big mouth. "Mr. Hayward, it could be that Simon really didn't notice the blanket. It smells so strong today because of the humidity. Up till today it's been cool and dry. Smells wouldn't have carried so much."

"Keith, are you trying to tell me that Simon wasn't drinking?"

"I don't think he was, sir. My room's right next door and I came up the same time he did the other night. I would have heard him if he got sick."

"That's right, you also excused yourself from evening activities on Tuesday, didn't you? Were you drinking too? Is that why you're standing up for Simon?"

"No, sir, I don't drink. It's just that I don't think you're being fair."

"Keith, I know what I see and I know what I smell. Simon heard the rules, just like the rest of you. He signed the paper, just like the rest of you. Now he's going to pay the price for his actions. I know you want to be a nice guy, but I suggest you accept reality."

Most of the time I think Simon is a real jerk, but I was positive that I would have heard him if he'd thrown up on Tuesday night. If I didn't stick up for him I knew I'd feel guilty if he got kicked out of school. "Mr. Hayward, I am sure that Simon was not drinking."

"Keith, have you ever heard the line from Shakespeare 'methinks the lady doth protest too much'? In this case, I think it is the boy who is protesting too much. You were drinking that night too, weren't you?"

"No! I told you, I don't drink." I was starting to get angry.

"Keith, I've heard that line from more students than I can count. Now, you haven't been in trouble before, and I don't have the proof that you were drinking that I have for Simon. If you drop the subject now, I'll let you off with just a warning."

"You can't prove that he was drinking. He says he wasn't. I say he wasn't and all you have is a blanket that could have been that way for weeks."

"Keith, I will not have a student make a fool of me. I know what I know. Now either you drop this or you pack your bags."

"I will not 'drop' the truth."

"Then pack. Now! Next week we'll talk about whether or not you'll be allowed to stay in our school."

Both Simon and I were sent home. Mr. Hayward, who led a group that wanted to tighten the discipline in our school, didn't want anyone to be able to say that he didn't practise what he preached.

When everyone else had returned from the trip, Mr. Hayward began the process for expelling Simon and disciplining me. It just wasn't right. I wrote letters to all of the people on the school board. I started a petition calling for justice for students. Several teachers told me that I was only asking for trouble. Many people began to think that I must be guilty since I was fighting so hard for someone who wasn't even my friend.

Tensions rose among the staff. Some of the teachers supported Mr. Hayward, while others said I had a point and that there wasn't enough real evidence to expel Simon. I got the feeling that all of the teachers wished I had just kept my mouth shut. I was taken off a student advisory committee to which I'd been appointed. Too many teachers were uncomfortable around me; I was no longer a good liaison between students and staff.

In the end, Simon wasn't expelled. There were enough people who felt that I'd raised too many doubts about the incident. But the trip for the next year was cancelled. Most of the kids blamed me. I had caused too much trouble for the teachers and given the trip a bad name, and all for the sake of someone nobody liked that much anyway. I went from being a popular kid whom the teachers liked to being an outcast who was labelled as a troublemaker.

I wonder if I should have kept my mouth shut. But I really don't believe that Simon was guilty.

Jesus and the Religious Leaders of His Day

The Priests

To be a priest in the Jewish religion, a man had to belong to a certain family: the tribe of Levi. The work of a priest was to offer grain and animal sacrifices, to decide what was clean and unclean,

Ruins of synagogue in Capernaum

and to preside over the great festivals at the Temple of Jerusalem.

Since there was only one Temple, only a few men could work as priests. All the other men in the tribe of Levi had to find other work, but they always remembered that they were part of the priestly family, and perhaps once in their life (by a sort of lottery system) they might be invited to preside at Temple worship.

The priests who worked at the Temple used to meet in a Council called the Sanhedrin. The President of the Council, or High Priest, at the time of Jesus was a man called Caiaphas (pronounced KY-a-fuss).

Gospel accounts of the death of Jesus show that these priests caused his death. He went on trial before the Council. They decided to take him to Pontius Pilate, the Roman governor, and demand that he be killed.

The gospels give two main reasons why the chief priests wanted Jesus dead. First, they were jealous of him. The priests had almost total authority in the Temple. They also got a lot of respect. When Jesus taught in the Temple, he took people's attention away from the priests. He also made them seem less important. Some people may have been more interested in having Jesus in the Temple than in having the priests there! When Jesus threw the money changers out of the Temple, he made people question the authority of the priests. After all, they were in charge of the Temple and they had allowed the money changers to be there.

Second, the priests were afraid of making the Romans angry. They thought that if Jesus had too many followers, the Romans would think that the Jews were getting ready to challenge Roman rule. The priests were afraid that if this happened, the Romans would destroy the holy places and even the Jewish nation itself.

Still, the Acts of the Apostles (6.7) tells us that many Jewish priests later became followers of Jesus.

Some groups in Jewish society were made up of people who joined together because they agreed on certain ways of thinking. (This happens today when groups get together to protest nuclear weapons or to lobby for business interests.) Let's look at a few of these groups.

The Pharisees

The pharisees were very strict religious thinkers. They were not priests, but many of them were rabbis. They believed that to be a good Jewish person, you had to obey the Law of Moses as perfectly as possible. They studied the Law very carefully to find out exactly what they were supposed to do.

Many of them were against Jesus because they thought he was wrong. When Jesus cured the man with the crippled (withered) hand on the Sabbath, the pharisees believed that he was trying to weaken the law. From the pharisees' point of view, Jesus was making something that was wrong look right. They believed that he had to be stopped.

When we read Matthew 23, it is easy to see why many pharisees did not like Jesus. Jesus calls them hypocrites and snakes! He says that by paying so much attention to the letter (the actual words) of the law, they destroy the spirit (the real meaning) of the law. Jesus tells these people who are so proud of being faithful to the law that they aren't really following the law. Maybe there was no greater insult to a pharisee than this.

Jesus' words might make you think that the pharisees were evil. This isn't true. In fact, their lives were shaped by their faith. When Jerusalem was destroyed by the Romans, it was the pharisees who re-organized the Jewish religion so that it could go on without priests and without the Temple. Without the pharisees, Judaism may not have survived. Many scholars think that Jesus criticized the pharisees so much because they came the closest to living life the way God wants people to live.

Some pharisees, such as Nicodemus and Paul, later became followers of Jesus.

Detail from Capernaum synagogue

The Sadducees

The Sadducees were even more traditional than the pharisees. They would not accept any teaching – even if it was in the Prophets or other scripture writings – unless it could be found in the Books of Moses (the first five books of the Hebrew Scriptures, which are known as the Torah).

One example of their attitude is found in Matthew 22.23-32. Many Jews believed that the dead would one day be raised back to life (resurrected). Jesus promised resurrection, but the Sadducees refused to hope for it because it is not found in the Books of Moses.

Jesus' teachings were usually much closer to the beliefs of the pharisees than to the beliefs of the Sadducees. The Sadducees followed the letter of the law even more strictly than the pharisees did. They were even more likely than the pharisees to be upset by Jesus interpreting the law in new ways.

The Sadducees were mostly rich people. Most priests belonged to this group, and so did many wealthy landowners and merchants. Most of them believed that it made sense for the Jews to co-operate with the Romans. They were very suspicious of anyone who threatened to upset the delicate balance between Roman authorities and Jewish ones.

The Scribes or Rabbis

In the time of Jesus, most ordinary people could not read or write. Professional readers and writers, called *scribes*, were very important people. They were the only ones who could teach others what was in the written traditions (such as the Scriptures).

The scribes were scholars who knew the Scriptures and Jewish traditions very well. Most of the scribes were pharisees in their way of thinking, so they taught from the pharisees' point of view.

People who learned from the scribes used to call them *rabbi*, a title of respect meaning *master* or *teacher*.

One place where scribes taught was at the synagogues. Although there was only one Temple (in Jerusalem), there was a synagogue in every little town. People would go to the synagogue on the Sabbath day to hear the word of God read from the Scriptures, to pray and sing, and to be taught by their rabbi.

Jesus criticized the scribes because they often thought more about their own image than they did about God and because their faith was all very public. He criticized them for being more worried about doing religious things that people would see than about justice and mercy, which might go unseen.

Many scribes fought against Jesus from the beginning of his ministry. What he taught was different from what they believed. He did not seem to value the things they valued. Jesus didn't seem to care about what people thought of him. He was doing things that made Judaism look ridiculous. He was spending time with known sinners and having contact with people with contagious diseases. He said that God wanted him to act that way!

Scribes were part of Jesus' trial and execution, and many of them were against the Christians after his resurrection.

Why Did Pilate Condemn Jesus?

Many of the religious leaders felt that Jesus was a real threat to Jewish faith and society. They wanted him out of the way, but they did not have the authority to sentence him to death. Only one person could do this: Pilate, the Roman governor of Jerusalem.

Jesus' trial before Pilate followed the standard process for judging someone who was not a Roman citizen. A few accusers brought Jesus before the Roman tribunal. They did not accuse him of breaking any laws. Instead, they said that he was doing many things that went against the proper authorities in Jerusalem. Those who wanted to see Jesus sentenced to death warned Pilate that if he let Jesus keep doing what he was doing, many Jewish people would start thinking of Jesus – not Caesar – as their king. They were hinting that Jesus was a threat to Caesar and should be sentenced to death for treason (trying to destroy the government).

Pilate asked Jesus to defend himself. He asked Jesus if he really thought of himself as a king. Pilate asked Jesus to respond to the pharisees' accusations that he was trying to weaken Roman authority. Jesus would not answer. Under the legal system in Jerusalem at the time, a man who was accused of a crime and did not defend himself was automatically found guilty.

Once a verdict of guilty was given, Pilate was free to choose a punishment to fit the crime. He could have Jesus flogged, as a warning to change his behaviour, and then release him; he could sentence Jesus to the most brutal of deaths – crucifixion; or he could choose something between the two.

According to the gospels, Pilate did not believe that the case against Jesus was so strong that he deserved to die. Pilate seemed to be ready to have Jesus flogged and then release him. But those who wanted Jesus dead put pressure on Pilate. John's gospel says they told Pilate that if he did not sentence Jesus to death, he would be supporting a rival to Caesar. Pilate might be charged with treason himself!

Pilate, either by his own choice or because he felt pressured by those around him, sentenced Jesus to death by crucifixion.

Martin Niehmoler was a pastor in the German Confessing Church who spent seven years in a Nazi concentration camp. His words remind all of us of the importance of speaking out on behalf of those who are victims of hatred and injustice.

First they came for the Jews
and I did not speak out because I was
not a Jew.

Then they came for the socialists
and I did not speak out because I was
not a socialist.

Then they came for the trade unionists
and I did not speak out because I was
not a trade unionist.

Then they came for me
and there was no one left to speak out
for me.

The Stations of the Cross

From the very beginning, Christians have tried to understand the suffering and death of Jesus Christ. As St. Paul guided us, Christians have always tried to be closely involved in the passion of Jesus. In Baptism, we die with him to sin and rise to new life for God; in the Eucharist, we proclaim Jesus' death; in daily life, we carry our cross and suffer with him. The Stations of the Cross is a prayer that helps us to meditate on the sufferings of Christ so that we may better know the love of God.

1. Jesus in the Garden of Olives
   Matthew 26.36-46

2. Jesus is betrayed by Judas and arrested
   Matthew 26.47-56

3. Jesus is condemned by the Sanhedrin
   Matthew 26.57-68

4. Jesus is denied by Peter
   Matthew 26.69-75

5. Jesus is condemned by Pilate
   Matthew 27.1-2, 11-26

6. Jesus is scourged and crowned with thorns
   Matthew 27.27-31

7. Jesus is made to carry his cross
   John 19.16b-17

8. Simon of Cyrene helps Jesus carry his cross
   Luke 23.26

9. Jesus meets the women of Jerusalem
   Luke 23.27-31

10. Jesus is crucified
    Luke 23.32-38

11. Jesus promises the kingdom to the repentant thief
    Luke 23.39-43

12. On the cross, Jesus speaks to his mother and his beloved disciple
    John 19.25b-27

13. Jesus dies on the cross
    Luke 23.44-49

14. Jesus is laid in the tomb
    Mark 15.42-47

8.2 What's the point of sacrifice?

The Dance Competition

Priscila Uppal

13 years old

I did it for my sister, Allison. I don't totally understand why.

It started at our dance class. Our teacher, Mrs. Gray, had entered our class in a competition in New York. Both my sister and I were desperate to go. When we reached home, we screamed and yelled as we asked permission from our dad. Allison was more excited than I was. She almost flipped when Dad agreed.

After a week, practices started. We went to a studio four times a week. At one of our dress rehearsals, Allison did a cat-leap, tripped and broke her leg. When we got home from the hospital, she locked herself in her room and cried. She would never be able to go to New York. And the worst part was that on that same weekend, Dad had to go away on a business trip. I went into my room and thought seriously about it. Poor Allison – alone all weekend with a broken leg. She had wanted to compete so much, and now her hopes were shattered. Right then, I decided I would stay home with Allison.

That weekend in December, I had a wonderful time. Allison did too. The look on her face when she found out that I would be with her was the absolute best competition anyone could win.

For the record, our dance class came in fourth.

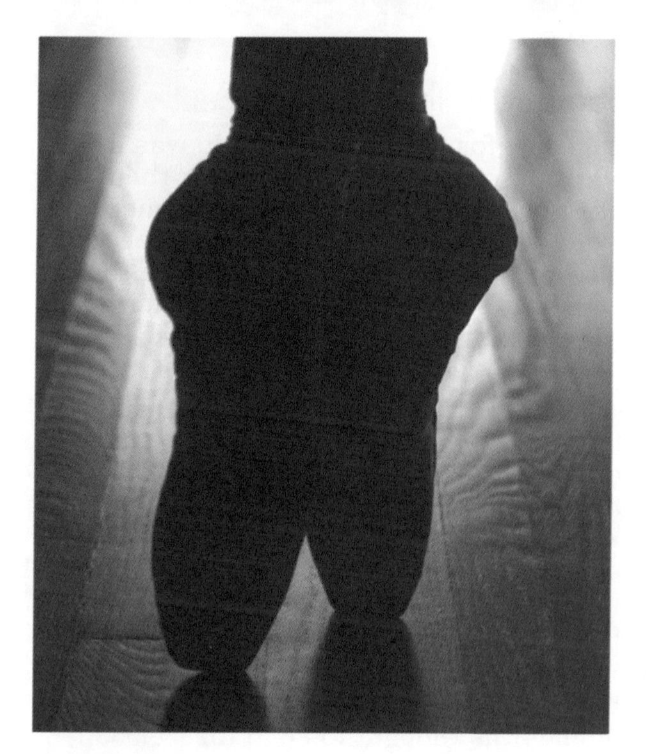

The Party

Jeff Stewart

13 years old

I had just gotten home from hockey practice when the phone rang. It was my buddy Jake.

"Mike," he said, "can I get a ride with you to that party at David's tonight?"

Just then it hit me. Oh, no! I was furious with myself. I could have just burst but instead I said calmly, "I'm not sure. I'll call you back in five minutes."

"Okay," he said, sounding puzzled.

I had promised my mom I would babysit my brother so she could go out with my dad. I had really wanted to go to this party and had been looking forward to it for weeks. But, on the other hand, I knew how much my mother needed a break. Not only does she take care of my little brother all day, she has also been helping old Mrs. Stelik next door ever since Mr. Stelik got sick. I picked up the phone and dialled Jake's number.

"Sorry, Jake, I can't make it tonight. I've already made plans to help my mother."

Reflection questions

1. What gifts did the young people give in the stories you read?
2. What value did these gifts have?
3. What does it mean to make a sacrifice?
4. Can you think of sacrifices that people have made for you? Why did they make these sacrifices?

What Is a Sacrifice?

A sacrifice is one person's gift of self to another. It is an act of love and faithfulness that draws people closer together. When we make sacrifices, we let go of our selfishness so we can get closer to someone else. Our sacrifices say: this relationship is so important to me that I am willing to let it shape the way I live my life. Personal sacrifices are needed in every healthy relationship.

Sacrifice is also part of a healthy relationship with God. We cannot grow closer to God unless we are willing to give as well as to receive. Throughout history, people have offered sacrifices to God as a way of saying that their relationship with God shapes their actions and their priorities.

Sacrifice in the Old Testament

Sacrifice for the Jewish people was a celebration of God's covenant with them. The covenant is a personal agreement in which God offers faithful love to the people, and the people agree to live faithfully as God's beloved children. The sacrifices were meant to express this relationship in a symbolic way.

When the Jewish people offered sacrifice, first they chose and killed an excellent animal from their flocks. Since the offering represented themselves, and since they knew that all life was a gift from God, they offered to God the best they had.

Second, the priest poured the animal's life-blood on the corners of the altar. Sometimes he also sprinkled some of the blood on the people. (The life of a person or animal was thought to be in their blood.) This action meant that God and the people were brought together when the life-blood

Doogie Dogma *(Catechism #609)*

touched both the people and God's altar. (Other words, such as "united," "joined in a covenant," or "reconciled," are sometimes used to mean "brought together.")

Third, all or part of the animal's body was burned on a fire at the altar of sacrifice. This meant that the sacrifice was a gift to God. The animal represented the people; the sacrifice showed that the people were dedicating their whole lives to praise God, to thank God, and to obey God.

Fourth, sometimes the people ate part of the sacrificed animal. This meant that God and the people were sharing a meal of friendship, or communion. The people were invited to God's table to be united with God and one another.

Jesus' Sacrifice

Why the word "sacrifice"?

Sometimes it is hard for us to find words to describe who Jesus is and what he has done for us. It's often hard to explain why Jesus suffered and died when, as the Son of God, he had the power to avoid death. The early Christians also found it hard to explain these things. In fact, they probably found it even harder than we do to express the meaning of the life and death of Jesus. For them, the idea of a God who could and would suffer and die was completely new.

As the early Christians looked for words to talk about their faith in Jesus, they thought about the sacrifices in the Old Testament. They began to understand Jesus' life and death as the perfect sacrifice that did what no other sacrifice was ever able to do. Let us look at what it means to talk about Jesus' life and death as a sacrifice.

Jesus gave himself willingly

After the Passover celebration, Jesus went with his disciples to a garden on the Mount of Olives to pray. Jesus did not want to die. When he was praying in the garden of Gethsemane before he was arrested, Jesus cried out to God. He asked God to spare him if this could be done without getting in the way of God's plan for humanity. Like most human beings, Jesus was horrified by the thought of dying. But he was willing to die if he had to choose between dying and rejecting God.

Judas Iscariot knew where Jesus and the others had gone. He also knew that for once, Jesus would not be with a large crowd. He could be arrested without there being a riot. Judas led the temple police to Jesus.

At least one of Jesus' followers was ready to fight to keep Jesus from being taken away. But Jesus did not want a fight. Jesus had taught that love was stronger than violence and hatred. He was willing to go without fighting because he believed what he had taught and because he trusted in God. Jesus was willing to die rather than use violence against those whom God loved. He was willing to die rather than give people reason to believe that right and wrong were based on power rather than on love, justice and mercy.

Jesus showed that he was willing to die rather than reject God by being silent when Pilate questioned him. If Jesus had tried to make Pilate believe that he was not trying to destroy the government, that what he taught did not hurt Caesar's authority, he would have been admitting that Caesar had a right to total authority. Jesus taught that all authority belonged to God – not to human rulers. Jesus was willing to die rather than place human authority above God's.

Jesus accepted the pain and shame of crucifixion

Crucifixion was the most degrading form of execution in Jerusalem at the time of Christ. It was used only for the most serious crimes. The Romans thought it was so horrible that Roman citizens were almost never crucified. The Romans believed that crucifixion was for "less valuable" human beings. The Jews believed that anyone who was crucified was cursed by God. We could say that a person who was executed on a cross paid the full price for human sin, since he was seen to be separated from both God and other people.

When a person was sentenced to death by crucifixion, he was flogged first.

Flogging, or scourging, meant whipping a person with a lash made of leather thongs attached to a handle. The leather thongs would cut into the victim's back, creating very painful wounds. Sometimes people died of these wounds. Other forms of torture were often added to floggings. In Jesus' case, after he was flogged, the soldiers twisted thorns into a crown and placed them on his head; then they dressed him in a military cloak – a costume for a king. The cloak and the thorn crown both humiliated Jesus and increased his pain. The cloak placed over his open wounds would make them hurt even more; when the cloak was taken off, it would pull on the wounds and make them bleed again.

After the soldiers had tormented their victim, they would place the horizontal beam for the cross on his torn back and force him to carry it to the place of crucifixion. The upright beam for the cross would already be standing in the ground. When the person to be executed reached the crucifixion site, his wrists were tied or nailed to the cross beam. The cross beam was then mounted on the upright beam. The victim's buttocks would rest on a small wooden peg, and his feet would be nailed or tied to the upright beam. The charge against a crucified person would be written on a sign that was hung either over his head or around his neck. The charge against Jesus stated that he was the "king of the Jews" – in other words, he was a threat to Caesar and guilty of high treason.

Since crucifixion did not hurt any of the vital organs, death was very slow and painful. Sometimes it took days for the person to die. A crucified person died of thirst, exposure and suffocation, as he became too exhausted to push himself up enough to fill his lungs. (Death could be speeded up by breaking the person's legs so that he could not raise his body enough to fill his lungs.) The crucified person was often given drugged wine to dull his awareness. When Jesus was offered such a drink, he refused it. He was completely aware of what was happening to him and yet he was still able to ask God to forgive those who tormented him.

The way Jesus died is significant because he gave himself completely. He held nothing back. Jesus endured all of the pain, both physical and mental, that human beings could give. He stayed faithful to God and never stopped loving other people.

Jesus offered the perfect sacrifice

The important part of any religious sacrifice was not the killing. It was the trusting of everything that one had, including life, into God's loving hands. Jesus did not just do this symbolically; he did it in reality. Jesus' whole life was an example of unfailing trust in God. In every moment of his life, he was the person God wanted him to be; he was always faithful to the command to love God and love his neighbour.

Jesus stayed faithful to God and was willing to love no matter how bad things got. He offered his love and faithfulness on behalf of all human beings. In Old Testament times, the sacrifice of an animal was the people's way of saying: "As this animal gives its whole life and holds nothing back, so we too wish to give our whole lives to God." But since the animal didn't give its life voluntarily, and since the animal could not give itself out of human love and faithfulness, the sacrifice of the animal was an imperfect connection with God.

Because the people could not make a perfect connection with God, animal sacrifices had to be offered over and over again. When Jesus allowed his life to be taken, he did it because he had so much love – even for those who hated him, and because he had such deep faith. He made the perfect connection between human beings and God. No other sacrifice could ever be as perfect. Because Jesus made the perfect connection between us and God, we say that he has redeemed us.

Now when we wish to reconnect ourselves with God, we do not need to offer a new sacrifice. We need to make the perfect sacrifice of Christ our own.

The Sacrifice of the Mass

We make Christ's sacrifice our own when we participate in the Eucharist

At the Eucharist, the events of Jesus' life – above all, his death and resurrection – are made present to us. We are with Jesus as he says: "This is my body which is given for you" and "This is my blood poured out for you." We are present as Jesus offers himself as the "lamb of sacrifice." We see his body broken and his blood poured out for us. We are also present when the disciples see Jesus alive. With them, we know that he has been raised up by God.

As these events are made present to us, we are able to respond to them and to allow them to shape the way we live our lives. We show most clearly that we are willing to be shaped by Christ's great sacrifice when we eat the bread that is now his body and drink the wine that is his blood. As we share the body and blood of Christ, we are closely united with Christ. Our very being is shaped by Christ. Christ offered himself to God as the perfect example of all that human beings can be. When we are united with Christ in the Eucharist, we commit ourselves again to being the very best that we can be.

The people of the Old Testament often ate some of the meat of the sacrifice as a sign of their new closeness with God. We receive communion not only as a sign of our new closeness with God, but also to make this new closeness a reality. When we eat and drink the body and blood of Christ, we stop being separated from God.

The Eucharist also unites us with one another. When we share in the one body of Christ, we join with others who have shared with us and we become the body of Christ. Once we have shared the body and blood of Christ, our unity is far more important than our differences. Together we now act for Christ in the world. Together we now become Christ's hands and feet and heart.

I give you thanks, O LORD, with my whole heart.

Psalm 138.1

8.3

Who's in? Who's out?

The Invitation

He sat and watched the others laughing and running. The tears would have streamed down his face if he had been a different kid, but he never cried. He just sat there with a scowl on his face and turned the same thought over and over in his head: "I could be dead for all the attention anyone has paid to me. I could be dead for all the difference I'm making to anyone or anything."

The bell rang for lunch. All of the kids started running toward the dining area. He just sat there. "What's the point? It's not like I'll have anyone to sit with anyway. I may as well just stay here." He scowled a little bit more and stared at the ground. He didn't even notice the other boy walking toward him.

"Hi! It's lunchtime, you know." The stranger sounded friendly enough.

"Yeah, I know. I'm not hungry."

"Come on. The food here's great. We have an extra seat at our table. Hey, do you play basketball?"

"Yeah." The scowl slid away. He stood up and went to lunch. After lunch he joined a bunch of the other kids on the court. The same thought kept going through his head: "These guys are pretty good. This place is going to be all right."

Who Are the Dead?

Did you ever ask yourself the question "What does it mean to be dead?" The obvious answer is that a person who is dead isn't breathing, his heart isn't pumping, and all brain waves have stopped. There is also the kind of "dead" when a person is still breathing and thinking but life just doesn't seem to matter. Finally, there is the sort of "dead" in which a person is dead to other people: neither one's actions mean anything to the other.

The boy in the story "The Invitation" felt this third kind of "deadness." He said that he "could be dead for all the difference [he was] making to anyone or anything." Many of us have felt the same way at times.

God made us to interact with other people. When we are cut off from others, we feel spiritually dead. We can be cut off from others when we are in the middle of a crowd, and we can be connected to others even if we are alone on a mountain or in our room. We are cut off from others when we do not love or feel loved. We are connected to others whenever love is part of our lives. We say that God is love. We also say that God is the source of all life.

Therefore, when we are cut off from love, we are cut off from life: we are dead.

As Christians, we believe that Jesus came to put an end to death – not only physical death, but also spiritual death. Jesus spent a lot of time with those whom society had left out. He offered love to those who felt cut off from love. We see Jesus' offer of love to all in his attitude toward lepers, prostitutes and tax collectors. We see it again in his descent to the dead after he was crucified.

In the first letter of Peter (1 Peter 3.18-19), we are told that after Jesus died on the cross, and before he rose, he went to the place where all those who had already died were waiting for the coming of the Messiah. The dead were seen to be away from the vision of God. They were kept apart from God's love. Jesus, however, brought God's love to all people, no matter who they were or how far from God they were.

Jesus is still inviting everyone to be one of God's people, to know life and love – no matter who they are or where they are. The only question is who will accept the invitation.

Will You Accept the Invitation to Life?

Jesus' invitation to us is an invitation to life and love. Jesus offers us God's love and acceptance. He promises us that no matter who we are, no matter what we have experienced, no matter what we have done, God loves us. Even if we do not accept God's love, God still loves us; but only when we accept God's love can we feel the life that comes from it.

Love is a funny thing. The only way we can really receive it is to give it. Love is a bit like a handshake or a hug in that way – to get one, you need to give one. If we want to truly experience God's love for us, we must love God. Jesus tells us that we love God by loving others, especially those who need love the most, those who feel cut off from love.

Unit 8 Summary Statements

- Jesus was crucified because he challenged the religious and social beliefs of his time.
- Jesus accepted suffering because to avoid it would have meant denying the truth and accepting injustice.
- Jesus challenges us to live the way God wants us to live even if that means we have to accept suffering. If we live the way God wants us to live we will love all people and treat them with dignity.
- A religious sacrifice is a sign of our commitment to God and our willingness to offer God the best that we have.
- Jesus' sacrifice is complete not because of his horrifying death in itself, but because he held nothing back. He gave himself completely.
- Christ's sacrifice occurred once and for all time. It was the perfect giving up of human life to God.
- We are invited to take part in Christ's sacrifice at the Eucharist.
- Christ's passion, death and resurrection are not just events from history. When we celebrate the Eucharist, these events become part of our present.
- We are called to follow Jesus' example and to give of ourselves for others.
- Christ's work of redemption – freeing us from sin – is for all people in all times and places. Jesus' invitation to life and love is offered to all people.
- We are called to share the good news with all people.
- Christ proclaimed God's eternal love and the redeeming power of that love even in death.

Key Terms

priests
pharisees
Saddducees
scribes
Pilate
crucifixion
sacrifice
Eucharist
Stations of the Cross
Sacrifice of the Mass
descent to the dead

Unit 9

On the third day he rose.
He ascended into heaven.

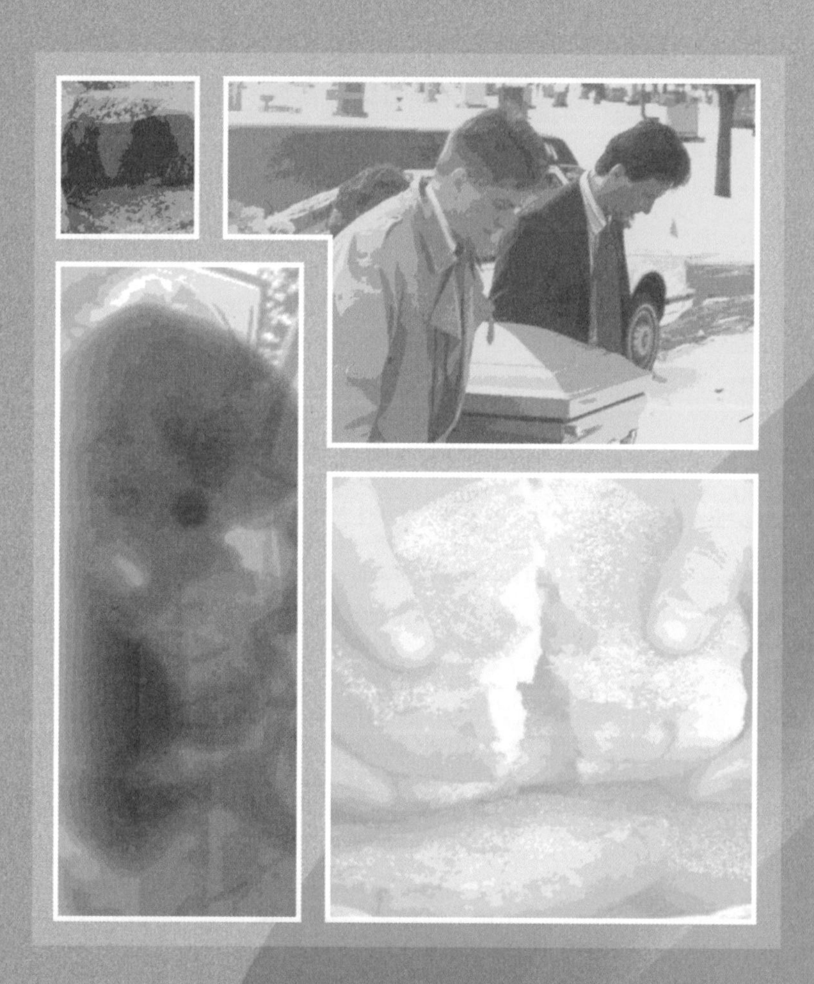

9.1 Is there hope?

Do You Believe in the Afterlife?

There is an old story about a conversation between two twins in their mother's womb. No one is quite sure what the names of the twins were. Let's call them them Maria and Andrea.

One morning, Maria rolled over and looked at Andrea. "It's getting really crowded in here," she said. "I'm getting uncomfortable and scared. We've been here for over eight months and I've heard that no one survives much beyond nine months." She kicked hard with both feet. "It seems crazy. Nine months, that's all you get. Then after that, birth!"

Andrea did as much of a somersault as she could. "Maybe it won't be so bad." She was one of those people who always liked to look on the bright side of things. "Maybe there's life after birth. Maybe what comes after birth is even better than this."

"You and your 'maybes'! Don't be ridiculous! This is all there is. Ask yourself, have you ever met anyone who's been born? Has anyone ever come into the womb and said, 'Hey, kids, birth is great. Don't worry, I've been there'? No, of course not. Because once you're born, you're gone. I don't know why we're even conceived if we're just going to be born."

"Well, I still think there might be something beyond birth. All this growing and changing that we've been doing must have a purpose." Andrea was quiet for a moment, then she asked, "Maria, do you think there's a mother?"

"Oh, don't tell me you believe in a mother too! You are so gullible! I'm not going to believe in some being I've never seen. Face it, one day there was a chemical reaction in the empty spaces of the womb and we were formed. There's no mother, no plan, no purpose; it just happened."

"But sometimes I'm sure I hear the mother singing to us. I'm sure there's something beyond you and me that's loving and protecting us."

"Andrea, you just don't want to face the pain of birth. You're making up all of these little fantasies in order to escape from reality. Birth seems to be a terrible thing, and there's nothing we can do to avoid it. Nothing you can say will make me think it's anything other than terrifying. When my time comes, I'm going to fight as hard as I can."

"Not me. I'm going to go quietly, with hope and trust in my heart."

"If you're so sure that birth is going to be a good thing, why didn't you try to be born earlier?"

"Just because I think that birth will be good doesn't mean that I don't think that this life is good. Besides, maybe there's a reason we are here as long as we are. I'll just wait and trust. Shh! Maria, did you hear that? I think it was the mother."

"I didn't hear anything. But I sure felt something. My head feels like it's being squeezed. I think I'm about to be born. Andrea, I'm really scared. What if I never see you again? Don't let me go."

"You have to go, Maria. That's the way life is. Try to be brave. The mother is helping you; I can feel it even if you can't. I'll see you in a while."

Where Is the Hope?

Maria's basic questions – "What's the point of life if it just ends?" and "How can I be hopeful when I'm faced with the loss of everything I hold dear?" – are questions that people have asked for thousands of years. These were the types of questions that tormented the disciples after Jesus' death.

For Christians, the answers to these questions are found in Jesus' resurrection.

When Jesus rose, we learned that death and loss are not all there is. Death and loss are not walls. They are doorways into new beginnings and new possibilities. We can be hopeful because Jesus has shown us that God's plan for us is eternal. The "point" of life is to move ever closer to God and the great joy and happiness that God offers us. Our losses do not need to stop us from moving closer to God. If we allow it, God will use our loss and our pain to draw us closer.

When Jesus appeared to his disciples after his resurrection, they could have chosen to be angry. They could have asked why they had to go through all of the pain, emptiness and despair if Jesus was going to rise again anyway. But Jesus helped them to understand that the pain and suffering couldn't be avoided. It was his death that had given them a new purpose, just as his resurrection would give them new courage and new hope. These stories of Jesus appearing after his resurrection remind us that God can help us find a purpose even in our pain. God offers us hope even in our fear.

Jesus Appears to Mary Magdalene (John 20.1-18)

Early Sunday morning, Mary Magdalene went to the tomb where Jesus' body had been laid. On Friday evening, there had not been time to properly prepare the body for burial. The Sabbath was beginning and no one was allowed to do any work. But now the Sabbath was over. The first day of the week had begun, and it was time to do all the things that were normally done to a body before it was buried.

Mary got to the tomb and saw that the stone had been rolled away. The tomb was open and empty. Her first thought was that someone had taken Jesus away. It was not enough to humiliate and execute him, they had to take from him even the respect that belonged to the dead. She ran to tell Peter and John: "They have taken the Lord out of the tomb, and we do not know where they have laid him." They ran back to the tomb with her, but of course Jesus was not there.

Peter and John returned home but Mary stayed by the tomb, crying. What could she do? What was left of this man whom she had followed, believed in and loved? What was left of her hopes and dreams? What would happen now that the one who had helped her put her life in order was gone? She had accepted forgiveness from this man believing that he spoke for God. But it seemed that God had cursed him. He had died on a cross and perhaps his body had been violated. Was she still forgiven? How could she go on? And now she didn't even have the rituals of preparing the body to help her get through this hard time. Mary wept.

As the tears ran down her face, she saw two angels sitting in the tomb. They asked why she was crying. Mary saw the angels. She answered their question, but their presence did not restore her hope. She kept crying. Someone else asked her why she was crying, asked if she were looking for someone. Mary thought he was the gardener. Maybe he knew where Jesus' body was.

Mary begged the man to tell her where Jesus' body was. She wouldn't cause any trouble. If the body had been moved because they didn't want him here, she would take his body somewhere else. Imagine all the thoughts and feelings that must have been going through her mind when she asked the gardener to tell her where Jesus was.

Then the man, whom Mary had thought was the gardener, spoke her name: "Mary." He knew her and she knew him! It was Jesus! He was alive! Just imagine what she felt at that moment. There was hope! There was a point to everything that had happened. Love and forgiveness had not failed!

Jesus told Mary that she couldn't hold on to him. He was alive, but his life was not exactly as it had been before. They couldn't go back to the way things were. New things had to be done. Jesus had to go to the Father, and Mary, as the first witness to the resurrection, had to go and spread the news. Jesus had called her to be the apostle to the apostles. Through Mary, Jesus entrusted the message of the power of God's love and forgiveness to his followers.

Jesus Talks to the Disciples on the Road to Emmaus (Luke 24.13-35)

Quietly, without hurrying, Jesus drew near to the two disciples on the road to Emmaus. They did not recognize him. In silence, he walked with them. Jesus knew that their hearts were filled with grief and disbelief. They were talking about Jesus' trial and crucifixion. Jesus was dead – he had been put to death. When he died, their hopes and their cause for joy had also died. Jesus knew the fear and frustration they felt now that some of the women in the group were saying that Jesus wasn't really dead. He understood why they were walking away from Jerusalem. But still he asked them, "What are you talking about?"

How do you think the two disciples felt? Did this stranger know nothing of Jesus of Nazareth, the man whom so many had come to trust? Did the stranger know nothing of Jesus' great failure? Didn't he know that Jesus had let himself be crucified?

The one they had thought would redeem them had hung on a cross and died. God's anointed one had failed. These disciples did not understand that this "failure" had ended death forever. Jesus tried to help them understand that the Messiah had to suffer and die in order to be the First Born from the dead and to lead others out of death. Jesus tried to restore their hope in God and their faith in their own judgment. They did not recognize or completely understand him, but they heard something important in what he was saying. The disciples asked Jesus to come in and eat with them. Even in their sorrow and doubt, they acted as Jesus had told them they should. They reached out to a stranger.

Doogie Dogma *(Catechism #646)*

When the bread was broken, their eyes were opened. They knew that this man – who had explained the word of God to them, who had given them a little bit of hope again, who had offered a blessing on their behalf – was Jesus. God had not abandoned them. Hope was not gone. And Jesus had made it clear to them that he could be heard in the words of Scripture and be seen in the blessing and breaking of bread.

Jesus and Thomas
(John 20.24-29)

Thomas was not with the others when they saw Jesus on the Sunday evening after his crucifixion. He did not believe that Jesus had risen from the dead. No one really knows why Thomas refused to believe his friends. Maybe he was afraid to trust again. He had believed once and been very disappointed. Maybe he didn't have the courage to hope. Or maybe Thomas was a person who always needed "proof," a person who never believed anything he hadn't seen with his own eyes. Maybe Thomas was the practical member of the group who always made sure that everyone knew what they were getting into before they decided to act. Maybe Thomas believed that there could be more than one explanation of what the others had seen. Whatever his reasons were, Thomas refused to believe that

Jesus had overcome death unless he could actually see and feel the evidence for himself.

Even though Thomas did not believe what his friends believed, he still spent time with them. He saw that it was important for the community to stay together, even if he didn't agree with all of its members about everything. Because Thomas did not give up on his friends, even when he was unsure about the faith that had brought them together, he was there when Jesus appeared to the disciples a second time.

Doogie Dogma *(Catechism #661)*

When Thomas did finally see the risen Lord, Jesus did not criticize him for his lack of faith. Instead, Jesus offered Thomas the proof he had asked for. Jesus also reminded Thomas that those who are willing to take risks and believe without concrete proof often find more happiness. They are blessed. Imagine the doubt and despair Thomas must have felt when he believed that Jesus was dead and that his friends were either imagining things or setting themselves up for a disappointment even greater than the crucifixion. Imagine how different that first week after Easter would have been for Thomas if he had accepted the resurrection.

Jesus loves and accepts us as we are. He does not condemn us for our doubts, but he does warn us that if we will not risk trusting in God, our lives will not be as happy as they could be.

Jesus Appears to the Disciples by the Sea of Tiberias[1]

(John 21.1-14)

Seven of Jesus' disciples were out fishing early in the morning. They had not caught a single fish. A man on the shore whom they did not recognize told them to cast their nets to the right side of the boat. (People who fish in that region today say that sometimes, because of their location, people standing on the shore can see a school of fish that those in a boat cannot see.)

[1] "The Sea of Tiberias" is another name for the Sea of Galilee.

Maybe the disciples did not find it strange that someone would call out from shore to offer help. But when their nets filled with fish, one of the disciples had a sudden insight. It had to be Jesus calling from the shore. Who else offered help so readily and in such abundance?

As soon as they recognized Jesus, Peter couldn't wait to be with him. Peter forgot the fish, forgot the boat and jumped into the water to swim or wade toward the shore. Imagine how Peter must have felt each time he saw Jesus and was reminded of the wonderful things God had done. Imagine how all of the disciples must have felt when they were reminded again that their hopes had become reality and God had won out over death. How might they have felt, knowing that God's love was stronger than anything else in the world, and that the one who embodied that love was standing with them offering them breakfast?

Jesus Commissions Peter in a Special Way

(John 21.15-19)

Jesus is the true "shepherd." He guides, protects and feeds his "flock" – God's children. When Jesus knows that it is time for him to return to the Father, he does not want to leave the flock without someone to guide it. Although he will no longer walk the earth as a human being, directly ministering to others, Jesus does not want direct ministry in his name to cease. Jesus commissions (or assigns) Peter and, through Peter, all of his followers, to continue the work Jesus had begun. We must do the work of reaching out in love and forgiveness to those who have been excluded, sheltering the weak, feeding the hungry, and searching out the lost.

Imagine how Peter must have felt when Jesus asked him three times, "Do you love me?" In repeating the question three times, Jesus was really asking Peter how sincere his love was, how much a part of Peter's self was love for Jesus. When Peter said to Jesus, "Lord, you know everything; you know that I love you," he was inviting Jesus to look all the way into his heart, to see into the very centre of his being, and to see that even there, Peter loved Jesus.

By connecting the question "Do you love me?" with the instruction to care for others, Jesus makes two things very clear. First, if we really love God, then we will care for others. Second, true care for others must be rooted in love. If we try to help others without love in our hearts, even our best intentions can end up causing harm.

As we listen to Jesus questioning and instructing Peter, we are called to question ourselves. Do we really love God? What are we doing to care for God's people? Are the "good" things that we do rooted in love for God and for other people? Or do we do what is good only when it makes us look or feel good?

A Meditation

God has created me to do some definite service for God.
God has given some work to me that has not been given to anyone else.
I have my mission. I may never know it in this life, but I shall be told it in the next.

I am a link in a chain, a bond of connection between persons.
God has created me for a reason.
I shall do good. I shall do God's work.
I shall be a messenger of peace, a preacher of truth in my own place...if only I keep God's commandments.

Therefore, I will trust God.
Whatever, wherever I am, I can never be thrown away.
If I am in sickness, my sickness may serve God;
in confusion, my confusion may serve God.
God does nothing in vain. God knows what God is doing.

God may take away my friends. God may throw me among strangers. God may allow me to feel desolate, allow my spirits to sink, hide my future from me – still God knows what God is doing.

Cardinal Newman (adapted)

Unit 9 Summary Statements

- The resurrection of Jesus is the central truth of our faith. We are a people of hope. We believe that as Jesus passed beyond death to new life with God, so shall we.
- The resurrection is the offer of new life in the face of death.
- The resurrected Jesus is the same Jesus, but he is no longer held back by the limits of time and space.
- Jesus calls us by name as he called Mary Magdalene.
- Jesus can be heard in the Scriptures and seen in the blessing and breaking of bread.
- Jesus calls us to begin again when we fail.
- Jesus calls us to celebrate our life with him by serving others.

Key Terms

resurrection
hope
Mary Magdalene
Thomas
Peter
commission

Unit 10

He is seated at the right hand of the Father. He will come again to judge the living and the dead.

10.1 Who's a winner?

The Swan's Children[1]

Once, a long time ago, a terrible storm swept the land. The rain pounded down upon the nest where a mother swan sat upon her eggs. The wind made the trees around her thrash wildly. The waters of the lake began to rise. The once quiet lake was now part of a raging river, but still the swan remained on her nest. The swan wanted to stay, but the rising water soon swept the nest out from under her. It was torn apart by the raging flood waters, and all of the swan's eggs were lost.

When the storm finally ended and the waters began to recede, the swan wandered along the edges of the lake near despair. She saw the broken remains of many homes. She saw the broken bodies of many of her friends, and she cried.

[1] Inspired by "The Birds," from *And the Master Answered* by Flor McCarthy, s.d.b. Notre Dame, IN: Ave Maria Press, 1985.

Because her head was bowed to the ground, she saw the egg and was able to avoid stepping on it. The poor motherless egg had survived the storm, but without a nest and someone to sit on it, it would not survive much longer. The swan gently picked up the egg and carried it away from the water. She placed it on some soft grass in the sun and then quickly began to build a nest.

She put the egg into its new home and warmed it with her own body. "I should go and see if there are others who need help," she thought. So as soon as she felt that the egg was warm enough to sit alone in the sun for a while, she set off around the lake to search for other motherless eggs that might need her help. She found two more, which she brought back and put with the first.

In due time, the three eggs hatched. An eagle, a loon and a pigeon all learned to call the swan "Mother." She loved and cared for each of them as if they were her own.

Then one day, while they were all still small, she placed them on her back and carried them to a high bluff overlooking a beautiful lake. "I must go away for a while," she said. "But before the cold sets in, I will return to take you to a wonderful place where the sun always shines and you will be safe from storms. Meanwhile, you must learn how to fly, because that is what birds were created to do. A bird who doesn't learn how to fly will suffer."

The swan flew off and the three were left alone. They were afraid, but they knew that the swan would never have left them alone if she thought they couldn't handle it. All three young birds were a bit afraid about flying. The bluff seemed awfully high. What if they made a mistake? They talked about their fears until night came; and then they huddled together for warmth and went to sleep. No one tried flying.

The next morning, soon after they awoke, the eagle announced that she was going to try flying. "I'm terrified, but if this is what birds are called to do, then this is what I must do." With that she closed her eyes, spread out her wings and ran off the edge of the cliff. The other two held their breath as she plummeted toward the earth. This wasn't going to work! But then the eagle flapped her wings once and slowed her fall. She began to glide slowly away from the cliff. Then she flapped again and climbed higher into the sky. In no time at all, she was plunging and soaring and turning tight loops. She made flying look easy.

The eagle returned to the cliff. "This is marvellous! You've got to try it for yourselves."

The loon took a deep breath and jumped into the air. In no time, he too was flying easily, riding the air currents down toward the water. When he reached the water, he began to swim and dive. He caught a large fish and flew with it back up to the top of the bluff. "Flying is magnificent! It's as much fun as swimming. Here, I've brought us some dinner."

Then both the loon and the eagle turned and said to the pigeon, "When are you going to fly?"

"I don't know. I don't think I will. It looks like a lot of work, and what if I fall?"

The loon and the eagle tried to convince the pigeon that flying was not really that much work and they were sure she wouldn't fall. But it was no use. No matter what the other two said to encourage her to fly, the pigeon always had an excuse for staying on the ground. Each day, while the others were off exploring the world, the pigeon waddled around the top of the bluff and pecked at the garbage left behind by the tourists who came to see the lake. Day after day, the eagle and the loon reminded the pigeon of what the swan had told them: "Birds were created to fly. A bird who doesn't learn how to fly will suffer." But the

pigeon saw no reason to learn to fly. She insisted that she could do just as well waddling, with less work and less suffering.

As the days passed, each bird learned and made choices about life. The eagle learned that when she soared over the lakes where young people were canoeing, she inspired them to paddle even harder. She decided to fly from place to place, searching out those who were ready to give up and encouraging them to try one more time. The loon learned that his voice brought comfort to those who were sad. He chose to travel from lake to lake, seeking out those who were lonely and soothing their pain with his song. The pigeon learned that if she made enough noise, people would throw food to her and she wouldn't have to do anything at all. She spent her days lying about and growing fat and never bothered to learn to fly.

The summer passed and the nights started to get longer. The three birds huddled close together during the night to keep warm. They wondered when the swan would return. Then, one evening, just as the sun was setting, they saw her coming toward them. All three cried out in joy.

"Ah, my three children. Are you ready to go to the land of the sun? Have you all learned to fly?"

"We have," the eagle and the loon sang out.

"What about you?" the swan asked the pigeon. "Have you used the wonderful gift of wings?"

"No. It seemed too hard and too dangerous. I've found that I can get plenty to eat right here. I like spending my days just sleeping in the sun. I'm so glad we're finally going to the land of the sun. I've been looking forward to this for ages."

The swan looked sad. "If you haven't learned to fly, you won't be able to come to the land of the sun. It is not a place for those who have done nothing but grow fat and lazy."

The pigeon began to whine and cry. "Let me come. It's not fair! You're misjudging me! I'm a good bird." But the swan simply turned and said to the birds, "Follow me."

The pigeon stood on the edge of the bluff and watched the other three fly off. "Who made her the judge of me, anyway? Just because I don't like flying, I don't see why the swan had to say that I wasn't allowed

to come to the land of the sun! It's easy to tell that the swan never thought of me as her 'real' child. I'm sure my real mother wouldn't have judged against me for a silly thing like not flying."

Judgment

Jesus is the light that lights up everything. His light is like that of a candle that gently lights up the corners of our lives, showing us to ourselves. Jesus' judgment does not fall on us like the glaring light of an interrogation lamp in a spy movie. It is not a light that makes us want to cover our faces and run and hide. Jesus' judgment calls to us like the light of a candle or a campfire. It is a light that calls us out of darkness and invites us into God's comforting presence.

Jesus' actions help us to understand the kind of light and the judgment he brings to the world. Jesus stands against those things that harm people. He replaces blindness with sight and deafness with hearing. He takes away deformities and diseases that destroy the body. He casts out those things that try to control people's minds. Jesus offers love and forgiveness in place of all that hurts us.

Jesus' judgment is to help people; it is against things and practices that hurt people. For example, Jesus might be against revenge because revenge makes people less able to love and to be creative. He will not condemn or be against a person who wants revenge, but he might say, "The wish for revenge must not be brought into my presence. You must choose – revenge or me." If a person chooses revenge, that person is not condemned by Jesus but will feel the effects of condemnation – separation from God – because he or she clings to things that are separated from God.

Although we may not see Jesus walking among us today casting out demons or telling people who are paralyzed to walk, the light of Jesus' judgment still helps us to recognize and move away from the things that make us act "blind" or "deaf" or "lame." Jesus' judgment still acts against those things that make people less than they could be. Even today, Jesus' judgment gently calls us to be the best people we can be.

Purgatory

We feel unworthy when we come into the light of God's presence. When the light of God touches parts of our lives, we see that they are dusty, or mouldy, or just not very nice to look at. Because parts of us do not look very good in the light, we know that we need to change to be at ease in the light of God.

Nothing that is harmful can survive if the light of God shines upon it. Some things that we cling to cannot exist in the light. If we wish to be completely in God's light, we must let go of those things. If we do not let go of them in life, we may need to let go of them after death.

We still have to work on our relationship with God even when we are dead. We need to be made pure so we can accept God's love completely. The Church calls this *purgatory*. This purification happens when God's light shines into the darkest corners of our being and helps us find and get rid of those things that keep us from having complete union with God.

Heaven

Complete union with God, a sharing in the love of the Trinity, is what we as Christians look forward to when we die. What is this like? We do not know, but we do believe in the resurrection of the body. That means we keep our identity even when we are dead. In heaven, God is fully present to us, and we are fully present to God and to one another.

To be in heaven is to have God's light shining through us so that there is nothing we need to be ashamed of, nothing we need to hide or be dishonest about, and nothing we need to fear within ourselves. To be in heaven is to know that we are completely loveable and completely loved. To be in heaven is also to be able to see God's light shining through others and to know that they too are completely lovable and completely loved.

Hell

We cannot be united with God unless we freely choose to love God; we cannot love God if we refuse to love our neighbour.

Hell is the state of final separation from God and our brothers and sisters. It is our choice. We are free to turn away from God. We are free to choose the darkness and all of the doubt, despair and fear that go with it. Some people may prefer to be in darkness than to accept truth and to change, which those who wish to live in the light must do.

In the darkness, we can believe whatever we like about ourselves and others. In the light, we see ourselves and others as we really are. In the darkness, we can convince ourselves that we have the right to control whatever we wish to control. In the light, we know that the world is beyond our control. In the darkness, we may pretend that others do not exist. In the light, we must see and work with others. Some people may prefer the false sense of power they find in the darkness. Some people may prefer hell.

Who's a winner?

Jesus began his public mission with a call to repentence: "Repent, and believe in the good news."

Mark 1.15

In order to repent, we must admit that all is not well in our lives. A winner is someone who recognizes his or her failings, and brings them in prayer before God.

"Believe in the good news." The winner recognizes that God loves us not because we are good, but because God is good. God's unconditional love – love that never stops no matter what we do – is a source of healing and strength. It draws us away from our failings. God's love helps us to be winners.

Choose a quiet time and place and become aware that you are in God's presence. Think about Jesus' message: "Repent, and believe in the good news." Ask God to help you understand what that means for you.

10.2

What's fair?

Judging Others

"Do not judge, so that you may not be judged. For with the judgment you make you will be judged, and the measure you give will be the measure you get. Why do you see the speck in your neighbour's eye, but do not notice the log in your own eye? Or how can you say to your neighbour, 'Let me take the speck out of your eye,' while the log is in your own eye?"

Matthew 7.1-4

Whom Do You Criticize?

Have you ever stopped to think about whom you criticize most often or what kinds of things make you most angry? If you're like most people, you probably get upset with people whose faults are a lot like yours, especially if they are faults you are trying to change.

People who are disorganized but who are trying to change may get very angry if someone else is disorganized. Someone who loses her temper easily may get very annoyed when other people lose their tempers, especially if she is being calm and patient at the time. A person who has cheated at games in the past but who is trying to stop may be quick to suspect and accuse someone else of cheating.

Jesus tells us that as soon as we feel like criticizing someone else, we should take a closer look at ourselves. Are we being critical because we really want to help the other person to be better, or because we want to show how much better we are? Most of the time, we criticize others because we think that if they look worse, then we will look better. We forget that hurting other people by ruining their reputations is a much bigger fault than most of the faults we criticize.

Only God Can Judge

Only God can see into a person's heart and know what he or she intends to do. Only God knows for sure if a person is really trying to do what is good or loving, or is choosing to be selfish and hurtful on purpose. In the beginning, God created human beings and saw that they were good (Genesis 1.31). Only God has the right to decide that any human being is not good; we do not have that right.

As far as possible, Catholics are called to assume that others are doing what they feel is right and good. When other people say or do something we do not like, we should try to understand it from their point of view. It is best to assume that they believed that what they were saying or doing was good, and that in their hearts they are good people.

Some actions are always destructive. They are wrong no matter what the reason is for doing them. We are called to speak out against those acts. But even as we condemn the acts, we must be careful not to condemn the people who do them. When we believe that someone is doing something wrong, we are called to challenge that person in a caring way. Even people who do things that we believe are absolutely wrong still deserve to be treated with dignity and respected as children of God.

When we observe one another, we tend to look only at the surface. God looks beyond the surface and into our hearts.

If you look at the picture below in the usual way, you will see a page of lines and colours. But if you do not focus on the surface of the page but relax your eyes and look beyond the surface, you will see something more. Only if you look beyond the surface will you be able to tell what this picture is really about. Only if you look beyond the surface can you see the heart of the picture. A person who only looks at the surface will misjudge the picture. Remember this the next time you feel like judging another person.

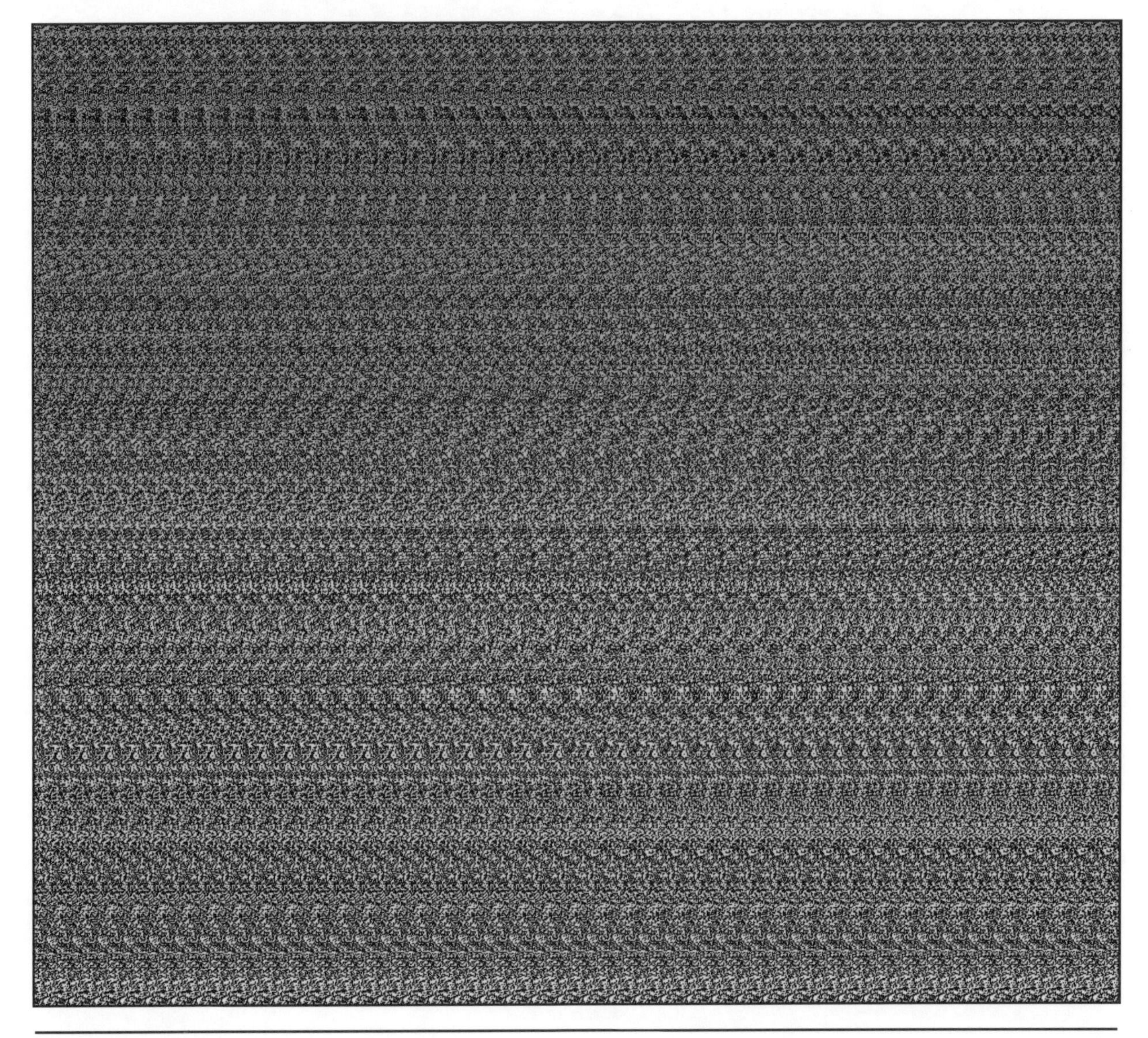

Two students' prayers

Lord, I know I'm not always kind and I don't always do the stuff I'm supposed to. But deep down in my guts, Lord, I know I'm a good kid. I'm sorry if I hurt you. I'll try to be as good as I can be. Please look beyond the surface and see the real me. Also, please help me to get my assignments done on time. Amen.

– Written by Scott M. (Grade 7)

Dear God,

I thank you for helping me make good choices. You help me get through the good and bad times. You help others that don't have the things I have. People who think that they've done something, think that you have stopped loving them. But you love and forgive and never forget them. Please help others and me to get through everyday life.

Thank you,

Brandy (Grade 7)

10.3 Does anyone really notice what I do?

The Good Deed

Squirrel and Snapping Turtle were called in to talk to God.

"I've been getting a lot of complaints about the two of you," God said. "It seems that you have both been doing many things to upset the other animals. Now, I believe that both of you wish to be good animals; so, before I decide how to respond to the complaints, I'm going to give each of you a chance to show me just how good you can be. We will meet again tomorrow morning. Between now and then, I expect to see some proof that you are trying to change."

Then the interview was over. Squirrel and Snapping Turtle were both sent back to their homes. Both of them were a bit nervous. Tomorrow was not far away.

As soon as he got back to his pond, Snapping Turtle went over to visit the Beaver family. The Beavers were building a new home, so Snapping Turtle thought that there was bound to be some sort of good deed that needed doing around their place. Sure enough, when he arrived, Snapping Turtle saw Mr. Beaver busily piling fresh wood on top of the new home while Mrs. Beaver had her paws full trying to enlarge the underwater entrance and keep track of all of the children at the same time.

"Good evening, Mrs. Beaver," Snapping Turtle called out in his rasping voice. "It looks like you have your paws full. Maybe I could help you. I'm quite good at digging in the mud. Why don't I enlarge your doorway so that you are free to look after the children?"

"Oh, Snapping Turtle, that would be a big help! It's so kind of you to offer. Is there something that I can do for you in return?"

"Well, there is one small thing," Snapping Turtle said slowly. "Do you think you could mention my kind deed to God? You see, I'm in a bit of trouble and I need to rebuild my reputation."

"It's the least I could do," Mrs. Beaver answered.

Later that evening, she and Mr. Beaver

talked about how lucky they were that God had chosen this particular day to speak with Snapping Turtle. Mr. Beaver made a special trip to say "thank you" to God and to tell God that Snapping Turtle was making an effort. Meanwhile, Mrs. Beaver made a special fish cake to send over to Snapping Turtle's house as a more personal sort of "thank you."

When Squirrel got back to his tree, he too was determined to find a good deed to do. He scurried over to the home of Mr. and Mrs. Chipmunk. They had had an unusually large number of children that spring, so Squirrel was sure that they would appreciate some extra help gathering food for the winter.

Sure enough, when Squirrel arrived he saw that the adult Chipmunks were looking very tired and frustrated. Mr. Chipmunk was wearing himself out running back and forth to their home with cheeks full of nuts. He would place the nuts by the door and then Mrs. Chipmunk would take them inside. But before she could get even half of the nuts inside, the little chipmunks would take and hide the others. They were too young to understand that this was not just a great game.

"Good evening, Mr. and Mrs. Chipmunk," Squirrel sang out in his fast, happy voice. "I can see that you have your paws full. Perhaps I can help. I would be happy to carry nuts to your house for you. Then, while Mrs. Chipmunk puts them away, Mr. Chipmunk could look after the children.

Perhaps he could play another game with them so that they are not tempted to hide the nuts."

"Oh, thank you, Squirrel," Mr. and Mrs. Chipmunk squeaked together. "We can't tell you what a difference that would make! We've heard that there's going to be an early winter and we're not nearly ready. Is

Doogie Dogma *(Catechism #1039)*

there something we could do to show you our appreciation?"

"Well, there is one small thing," Squirrel said slowly. "Do you think you could mention my kind deed to God? You see, I'm in a bit of trouble and I need to rebuild my reputation."

"It's the least we could do," the Chipmunks answered.

Later that evening, Mr. and Mrs. Chipmunk talked about how lucky they were that God had chosen this particular day to speak with Squirrel. Mr. Chipmunk made a special trip to say "thank you" to God, and to tell God that Squirrel was making an effort. Meanwhile, Mrs. Chipmunk made a special acorn cake to send over to Squirrel's house as a more personal sort of "thank you."

The next day, both Squirrel and Snapping Turtle felt fairly confident when they once again found themselves sitting before God.

"Well," God said, "you've both made an effort to be helpful. However, Snapping Turtle has pleased me most."

Squirrel started to chatter angrily. "What do you mean? How was his effort any better than mine? Are you saying that helping Beavers is better than helping Chipmunks just because Beavers are bigger?"

"Now, Squirrel," God laughed, "you know I wouldn't say something like that. I love all animals equally. No, Snapping Turtle did more than help the Beaver family."

"I did?" Snapping Turtle looked puzzled. "What did I do?"

"Yesterday, on your way back from the Beavers' house, you picked up an old bottle that someone had thrown into the pond."

"Oh, yeah, I remember. I hate seeing trash around. I figure we all need to do our part to keep things clean. But what's so wonderful about picking up a piece of garbage when no one even knows I did it?"

"Well, you see, that particular piece of garbage was blocking the back entrance to the Otters' summer home. They don't have the strong jaws that you have so they had been unable to move it.

"Now, when Mrs. Otter saw that the bottle had been moved by someone unknown, she was very grateful. In fact, she was so grateful that she decided to try extra hard to do something thoughtful for someone else that same day. That's why, even though she is terrified of geese, she found the courage to wake up a young goose who was sleeping under a bush and tell him that if he hurried, he could still catch up with the flock that had accidentally left him behind. The goose was so impressed by the thoughtfulness of an otter who was a complete stranger that he was inspired to go out of his way to help a sparrow who was caught in a bush. The sparrow, in turn, helped a field mouse find a lost baby.

"And so it went. All through the evening, your kind deed, done without thought of a reward, passed from animal to animal. Each of those good deeds I credited to the animal who did them and to you, for without you they would never have been done."

"Do not let your left hand know what your right hand is doing" (Matthew 6.2-4)

Jesus said, "So whenever you give alms, do not sound a trumpet before you, as the hypocrites do in the synagogues and in the streets, so that they may be praised by others. Truly I tell you, they have received their reward. But when you give alms, do not let your left hand know what your right hand is doing, so that your alms may be done in secret; and your Father who sees in secret will reward you."

Unit 10 Summary Statements

- Jesus' judgment is the light coming into the world – the light that makes the blind see, the deaf hear and the lame walk.
- Jesus' judgment is like the light of a candle that gently lights up the corners of our lives, showing us to ourselves, calling us out of darkness into light.
- Jesus came not to judge, but to give life. We judge ourselves when we accept or reject his gift.
- God's judgment calls us to conversion.
- Heaven, hell and purgatory are reflections of our ongoing choices.
- We will be judged in the same way that we judge others.
- Although we cannot judge the hearts of others, that does not mean that we should ignore actions that are wrong.
- We are called to follow Jesus' example and to invite others to live life more fully.
- Jesus challenges us to show special concern for those who do not like us or whom we do not like.
- God sees and rewards what is done in secret.
- Goodness may not always be recognized by others or even by ourselves, but God always sees it.
- We are called to bring the light of Christ to all that is in darkness.

Key Terms

judgment	Hell	conversion
Purgatory	repentance	true goodness
Heaven		

Acknowledgements

Acknowledgements

Believe in Me, Student Text, is the Year 7 catechetical resource of the "We Are Strong Together" © series, written and produced by the National Office of Religious Education of the Canadian Conference of Catholic Bishops, Ottawa, Canada.

Approved by:

The Episcopal Commission for Christian Education, Canadian Conference of Catholic Bishops

Project Specialists, Youth Portfolio:

Pam Driedger
Jonas Abromaitis

Editing and Writing Specialist:

Anne Louise Mahoney

Resource development group:

Jonas Abromaitis, Rosalie Carroll, Hélène Coulombe, Rev. William Derousie, Carol Donahue, Pam Driedger, Douglas Finbow, Jane Gray, Catherine Gross, Alan McLelland, Carole Murphy, Loretta Nurse, Catherine Reschny, Lynn Selinger, Deirdre Thomas, Mike Thorson

We acknowledge with gratitude the National Catechetical Advisory Committee on Youth, pilot teachers, co-ordinators, school boards, diocesan offices, and others throughout Canada who contributed to the development of this resource.

Anthony de Mello, S.J. Used by permission of Doubleday, a division of Bantam Doubleday Dell Publishing Group, Inc.

Martin's Story, excerpt from *From Desolation to Hope* Copyright © 1983, revised 1990, Stimulus Foundation. All rights reserved.

In His Image, text and illustration © William Zdinak 1973.

Art and Design

Creative Art & Design, Publications Service, CCCB

Cover Art & Illustrations:

Ron Tourangeau

Illustrations:

Chris Radisch – 38, 70, 93

Cartoon drawings:

Caili Woodyard

Photographs:

AP/Wide World Photos – 33-34
Jonas Abromaitis – 90, 154-155, 182
Tim Barnwell – 100
Bernie Carroll – 14, 58, 114, 165
Cirque du Soleil – 26
Concacan Inc – 87, 99, 100-101
DIRE – 57, 94, 98
Tom Day – 72
Pam Driedger – 52, 130, 132-133, 147, 149, 169
Glasgow Art Gallery – Salvador Dali, Christ de St. Jean de la Croix – 100
Joyce Harpell – 87, 91, 94, 109, 126, 150, 152-153, 157, 160-161, 171, 175
Tom Hocker – 97
Royal Ontario Museum, Toronto – 39
Secretary of State – 178
SKJOLD – 6, 11-12, 15-16, 36, 46-47, 50, 56, 61, 65, 77, 79, 80-81, 86-87, 95, 100, 104, 106, 111, 113, 116-117, 119, 122-123, 125, 140, 144, 164, 168, 185-188, 190-193
Ron Tourangeau – 180-181
Bill Wittman – 10, 12-13, 18, 37, 42, 47-48, 54, 64, 67-68, 73-74, 76, 82, 88, 108, 128-129, 140, 155, 162-163, 179

Printed and bound in Canada by:

Tri-Graphic Printing (Ottawa) Limited

Published by:

Publications Service, Canadian Conference of Catholic Bishops,
90 Parent Avenue, K1N 7B1
Ottawa, Ontario, Canada

2nd printing, 1997
3rd printing, 1999

ISBN 0-88997-314-8

Legal Deposit:

National Library of Canada, Ottawa

icene Creed

We believe in one God,
the Father, the Almighty,
maker of heaven and earth,
of all that is seen and unseen.

We believe in one Lord, Jesus Christ,
the only Son of God,
eternally begotten of the Father,
God from God, Light from Light,
true God from true God,
begotten, not made, one in Being with the Father.
Through him all things were made.
For us men and for our salvation
he came down from heaven: